Dedication

This book is dedicated to every person that I have met in my life: the ones that I treated poorly, and the ones that treated me poorly; the ones that showed me compassion, especially the people of twelve-step rooms, and the ones that have led me to my solutions. Thank you to all of my professors at City College of San Francisco for willingness to spend time on me with my writing, for until a couple of years ago I couldn't even read. The two professors I want to thank most are Professors Loren Bell and Bill Graves. There is also a professor at San Francisco State University, Michael Sudduth, that gave me insight on Neoplatonism.

All of these people spent time with me, encouraged me and read my work to give me their input. The people gave me their input on my writing, like my friends Kelly Hammack, Sinead Jonaidi, and Charlotte Tanaka. To my grandmother for being the first person to love me unconditionally, and my wife Elaine for the love we have for each other. But I truly want to thank the two first teachers that helped me in my life. The first teacher that I told everything to, Patrick Fleming, and my teacher Jody Foster at Discovery Academy, who encouraged my poetry writing when I could barely read.

Prologue

I'm writing this book because I am an alcoholic, and unlike almost every other alcoholic I have met in AA, I always knew I was an alcoholic. I have heard more than anything else that alcoholics couldn't acknowledge their alcoholism. It was one of the few things that I couldn't relate to. One of the main premises in recovery is that we were incapable of being honest with ourselves. I always knew I was an alcoholic. I just couldn't admit the rest. This book is about how I had to be honest with myself about what it means to love and be loved, and what the driving force in my life before and even after I quit drinking was: fear.

Every human has a problem with fear, and fear is why there is so much conflict in the world. With alcoholics, and the people affected by this disease, fear dominates their lives. My whole life was dominated by fear. This fear was shown to others as an enormous amount of anger, which manifested into a brazen ego. It was as though I came across as fearless. I hid it all quite well.

I remember asking two people I looked up to in recovery the first time I had a year sober if they thought I was an angry person. When I asked them, they both laughed as hard as they could. I could see my alcoholism, but I had no ability to see my anger, and that was because I could never acknowledge my fear.

This fear came to me at an early age. As a child, I got hospitalized at the age of thirteen. I spent my fourteenth birthday in the psych ward for homicidal and suicidal tendencies. I was quickly shipped to a disciplinary boarding school. It was at that boarding school where I learned to hide my fear from everyone, including myself.

The first day I got to that school I was terrified because everyone started to pick on me for no reason. After about a month there, I snapped. I went from someone that was picked on, to someone that picked on everyone else. It was at that school that I developed oppositional defiance disorder.

Oppositional defiance disorder means that if there was anyone in any type of authority situation whatsoever I had to stand up to them and defeat them. I was really good at it too. I had the doctor who owned the school, Dr. Thorn, scream and yell at me and tell me to fuck off. I had some of the counselors get violent with me just from what I said to them. I had the head of the female counselors crying in the front office that she wasn't fat. I was the one confined, but I proved to everyone else who was in charge of me that they were powerless. I have never met anyone who was able to make people as angry as I could. I got an enormous high out of doing this. This behavior was harder for me to give up than my addiction to drugs and alcohol, and I had an extremely hard time getting sober.

When I was at that boarding school, I started to have simple, partial, and partial complex seizures. The doctors at that school told my mother I was doing it for attention. Because of the seizures when I got home I wouldn't drive a car and get a job. That's why my mom kicked me out of her house. When she did kick me out, I moved in with my uncle in San Francisco.

In San Francisco, I got diagnosed with epilepsy and bipolar disorder. I went to AA because my doctors said I would die of seizures if I didn't quit drinking and using drugs. It was fear that got me into the rooms of recovery. Yet it was my fear of life that kept me from getting sober right away as well.

After drinking and using in San Francisco for ten years and going to AA every day for about eight, even when I was drunk, I finally got sober and stayed sober. My sobriety date is one day before my birthday in 2006.

This book isn't about my alcoholism, but the fear of being alone. I needed someone to make me feel complete, but I couldn't realize that no one can do that for me. Even with my antisocial disorder I always had the fantasy of love in my mind. The problem was I never had a good definition of what love was.

Despite all my behavioral issues, there was this part of me that was more companionate towards people that were suffering than most people I knew. Love was something that has always been in me. I've even had people tell me that I've saved their lives just by taking time to see how they were and showing compassion for them when no one else would. There was this one guy who hated me, and when he was dying in the hospital I held him and let him cry in my arms. It was as though I needed to know I couldn't get hurt. If they were suffering, then I knew I could be there for them.

When I met Jessica, I had just gotten out of a crazy relationship that I had a hard time detaching from. I went from one sick person to another, and my insanity continued. Since the relationship with Jessica, I have realized that I am powerless over more than just alcohol, which everyone is powerless over, in my opinion. We are all powerless over what we need to learn in this lifetime. This is because fear is something that controls most people, and fear is something that most people are blind to.

In my life, I have had a fear of not being worthy or enough. This was the fear that permeated my life and existence. I had gotten it as a child, and I took that pain into my adult life. In my adult life, I always looked for someone to fill this void within me. I wanted what every person wants. I wanted to be loved and accepted.

I had this big mental complex that I was extremely stupid because I didn't do well in school growing up, and I could barely read because of my learning disabilities. I also got diagnosed with Asperger's when I was in San Francisco. Asperger's was something they thought I had as a child, but my mother refused to believe it because she didn't want to take it as though there was something wrong with a child that she created.

When I was a kid they gave me an IQ test because I was doing so poorly in school. I tested in the top 5%. Parts of my brain are developmental, and in other parts of my brain I am extremely intelligent. I am even a savant with my memory and the way I am with numbers.

Like I stated earlier, kids that have had oppositional defiance disorder have antisocial tendencies as adults. Antisocial in psychiatric terms means that they will hurt people. I did it with my words. I have had doctors and psychiatrists ask me how I think of the insults that I think of. I had one psychiatrist tell me I was a genius with the way I could think of these creative insults so quickly. I would make them particular to each person. I could see what was wrong with anyone in a split second and let them know in a way they'd never have heard before.

Every insult in this book is something that I actually said to someone just off the top of my head. The solutions are my own ideas, which have been inspired and pieced together by AA and the people I looked up to in recovery and history. I also imagine that any conclusion I've come to in this book has been thought of before because I believe that all the answers for everything in this universe are within each one of us. All the answers being in us is something I got from Plato, and it has been shown to me through my life's experiences.

I don't speak for anyone in recovery, and most of the ideas in this book aren't text book recovery ideas at all. A lot of people in AA don't like the conclusions that I have come to because they are outside of the literature. People in recovery say, "keep it simple," "the program is within the first 164 pages," or the one I hate the most, "figure it out isn't a slogan." It's as though they think ignorance is a solution. They should all realize there is only one evil in this world and that is ignorance. I need to do soul searching. Soul searching is never simple, the answers to life manifest in infinite different ways, so figure it out. That is the only slogan that truly matters.

There is another saying, "self-knowledge avails us nothing." I disagree with this more than anything else. I believe that the only thing I can ever know is myself. Everything else in this world is just probability and speculation. The words, "I don't know" are the only words that will honestly answer every question there is about the outside world. If I want to solve my behavior and the conflict in my mind, it is only about self-knowledge, and the self is the only thing I can ever truly know anyway.

This book is about the answers I have found in my life. These answers have taken me from an extremely angry person, who couldn't count how many times tried to kill himself and harm other people, to someone who loves life today. I have gotten this only by trying my best to love and accept everyone else, and searching for the answers within me.

I still have a very hard time with people because of my mental and psychological disabilities. I have the aspects of nine different mental and psychiatric disorders, yet I don't fit any one stereotype completely. This is something that put a wedge between me and everyone for a long time. It is something that, to this day I am still working on overcoming.

Happiness is my goal, and when it comes to myself the answer is a paradox. This paradox is that I'm perfect the way I am and there is always room for improvement. God created each one of us in a certain way. We are the way we are because we need to learn the lessons of life that are particular to this lifetime. That is what tells me I am the person I am meant to be.

What we need in life to be happy is a good definition of love. I define love today as wanting the best for someone and taking the necessary steps to carry that out. This is something I try to practice with everyone today, and no matter what I, or anyone else, does or goes through, I know it is for a reason. This definition has taught me a lot, and as said in the Prayer of Saint Francis, "to love is to be loved."

The awakening that I have in this book is immediate, but in real life it started with the clarity of the first Al-Anon meeting, and it has sprung from there. Today I try as hard as I can to be a better person: A person who has the goal of trying to show compassion for everyone. It has only been through the rooms of recovery that this goal has been able to be possible.

To make it clear, all the names in this book are changed besides mine. I am respecting the anonymity of everyone else in my life because I realize it is not up to me to divulge anything about anyone else.

Chapter 1: The Way I've Always Been

I was riding the 45 bus as I was on my way to an AA meeting in the Marina in San Francisco. It was the town I lived in at the time. Alcoholics Anonymous is where I went to get sober. I'm someone that couldn't get sober while I was going to meetings for about the first eight years. I had a very hard time getting any type of recovery, but at the time of this story I had a little over two years of continuous sobriety.

It was Friday night. I always went to the same meetings. Everyone in recovery does this. We need to develop a community. Some meetings are really annoying, and others I enjoy. I've been told that meetings are like bars: you have to find the ones you like and fit into.

I was sitting in the handicapped seating. That was where I always sat because of my epilepsy. I had been having seizures every day of my life since I was fifteen. They weren't dangerous any more, but sometimes they would cause me to lose my consciousness and forget everything for about a half an hour. That was why I never wanted to stand on the bus. I also hated riding in the back of the bus. All the ghetto people rode in the back of the bus.

The bus got to another stop and opened its doors to let people on. Some big buff guy was one of the people that got on. He entered through the rear door. He had a lap dog with him. There was also this tranny that I knew, Stephany, who was pretty chubby. She was with him too. It looked as though they were going out or something. With the dog that he had in his arms, he sat in the seat right next to me.

"I hate dogs," I muttered to myself.

I always had a soft mutter. It wasn't that I was crazy — well not anymore. It was just that I have always thought words. While most people think in pictures, I think in words. My mind has also always been a very busy place, and I've needed to be able to process everything I was thinking out loud. It helped me to think clearly. I knew it was weird and off putting, so I'd always tried to do it quietly to myself.

Right as he sat down next to me the dog started to sniff me. "Would you sit somewhere else with that dog? It's starting to sniff me and I don't appreciate it." I said this in an intense snarl so I could get my message across.

"Hey, I get to sit anywhere on this bus that I like. It's a service animal."

"Listen, something stinks, and I actually can't tell which one of you it is, so can you at least scoot over?" I asked, raising my voice.

Then Stephany sat down on his other side and took the seat I wanted him to move to, so I raised my voice even louder and said, "I can see you stroke that furry thing just like you do the pecker which is under that dress!" I was staring him directly in the eyes.

"Hey, don't talk about my wife that way, you prick!" I guess he'd seen me in the rooms of AA before so he asked, "Who is your sponsor? Does he know that you talk to people like that?"

"He knows! But it is all about progress not perfection! I'm still putting a lot of effort into it! Do you know that grown men with lap dogs for emotional support are crazier than schizophrenics?"

"Hey man, I have a one bedroom in the Embarcadero! What do you have?" He said this as though he was talking down from some rich pompous cloud.

I stood up and yelled at him as I pointed my finger directly at Stephany, "Well I bet you spend a lot of money on food too, with that fat ho' sitting next to ya!"

Stephany was sitting there stunned in horror. Then the guy screamed, "Screw you! Don't talk to her that way! That's my wife! Don't talk to her that way!"

"I know she has a dick under that skirt because a Buddhist monk fucked her in that ass, and the only thing she wanted to do after that was suck on it!" This was all true. The monk bragged to a lot of people about it at the Castro Country Club.

I went on, "It is quite amazing too because monks aren't supposed to have sex, but I guess no one could resist that chunk! The only difference between you and him is that you wanted a kiss afterwards! I know that fat slut, and that must be the very reason you love her so much!"

"I could beat your ass! I am going to beat your ass next time I see you!"

The bus was coming to another stop, and because they were so hysterical and scared by what I said to them, they both got up and ran off that bus. I sat back in my seat. He had one arm waving in the air and the other clenching his dog. Wham! Wham! Wham! He was pounding the bus's window which was right behind me. I just raised my middle finger up in the air without looking. Then I slowly turned around and saw him still screaming as they both ran down the street. As the bus was taking off I blew him a kiss and then waved and goodbye.

No one messes with me, and when they do, I always get the last word. I've never been too physically tough, but no one, I mean no one, ever wins a battle of words with me. Even when they are beating the crap out of me, they would always walk away angry.

Chapter 2: Love at First Sight, Just Like Always

I had just gotten off the bus and was headed to the meeting. I walked in and got my seat. I had my headphones on so I didn't have to talk to anyone. I was bouncing up and down to my headphones, just sitting in my chair waiting for the meeting to start.

That was when I saw her. She was a beautiful girl who looked just about my age. I had just turned thirty. She had silky long blond hair with a touch of brown roots. I could tell it was dyed, but it came across as very attractive. She also had these big brown puppy dog eyes. I've always been attracted to shorter women, and she was at the perfect height of about five feet or so. She was wearing the cutest pink sweater which matched the blush on her cheeks perfectly. She had white jeans that fit her ass, and for a short girl she had extremely large tits.

My heart reached out to her right there, but I was also someone that was extremely scared of getting rejected, so I just kept my music on. I still couldn't help but stare at her. I wanted to talk with her. The only problem was that I had never been able to make the first move.

I would always develop these instantaneous crushes on people before I even knew them. I would see someone that was adorable and my eyes would dictate to my heart, then heart would control my mind. I was convinced I was in love with a person before I even got to know them.

The meeting had just started so I took off my headphones and I stared at her from across the room. I was wishing I could be with her.

My friends always told me I am more of a lesbian because every time I have sex with someone all I can think about is marriage. Be it a man, woman, or a tranny, I would never have had the ability to control my need for who I wanted.

At the beginning of the meeting, when they asked for newcomers to AA, I heard her say, "I'm Jessica, and I'm an addict."

"I don't care if she's a newcomer. I want her anyway," I muttered.

In AA, everyone calls dating a newcomer thirteen stepping because there are only twelve steps. You are not supposed to date someone when they are brand new. People that are new to recovery have too many problems. Dating newcomers is something that is really looked down upon. It truly doesn't matter, because a lot of people do it anyway. A lot of people in recovery are convinced they are more spiritual and moral than they truly are. I just sat there looking at her and dreaming.

I tried looking away, but my eyes were locked on her. I could only glance somewhere else for a couple of seconds, and then my eyes were pulled right back to her by something that was beyond my control. I felt as though she could tell because she kept glancing back at me each time. I was embarrassed because she must have known. There was nothing I could do. It scared me to be so vulnerable.

The speaker sucked anyway. It was a speaker/discussion meeting, so the speaker told their story of what it was like, what happened, and what it is like now. Some people are amazing speakers, but they are few are far in between. Most people in AA suck at speaking. It's not like there are really any professional speakers that come to AA. We're just alcoholics that are sharing our stories with each other so we can stay sober.

If you've been to one meeting, you've been to them all. I enjoyed going to meetings especially because I always shared from the floor. The only ones where I didn't were the ones that I didn't get called on. Since I've stayed sober, and because people like what I says so much, I get asked to tell my story more than most people.

When the speaker was done with their story they'd picked the topic. He made the topic the Second Step: "Came to believe that a power greater then ourselves could restore us to sanity."

He spent the whole time calling on other people. It was staring to piss me off, but I knew he couldn't ignore me for the whole meeting.

Finally, he said, "Justin."

"My name is Justin and I'm an alcoholic"

The room responded with, "Hi, Justin."

"I was a chronic relapser for a very long time. I would get a couple of days and use again. I did that for about the first eight years of my attendance at meetings. No sponsor I had would ever take me past the First Step because I would never stay sober. When I got here I hated God. I hated God because of the boarding school that I went to. It was in the middle of Provo fucking Utah!" I shouted in disgust.

"None of the kids were Mormon, but the missionaries would come on the weekend to convert all the kids. It was forty thousand dollars a year back in the early '90s. None of the parents knew what the people who ran the dump were doing. It was called Discovery Academy. We all called it Dick Suck Academy."

Everyone laughed.

"I would say the parents probably didn't care. They didn't know what to do with their children. They converted one kid whose last name was Jones, so we all called him Jesus Jones."

The room giggled again.

"It sucked! I was raised Catholic, but my family never really shoved it down my throat. Church was just the longest hour of the week.

"It says in the *Big Book of Alcoholics Anonymous* that defiance is one of the key characteristics of an alcoholic. Well, I was defiant way, way, way before I started to drink. As a child I developed oppositional defiance disorder, so I fought everyone, including God.

"There's this story in the Book where some guy has an epiphany when he asks himself if all the religious people in the world could be wrong? He says to himself, 'who am I to say there is no God.' My response to that was: who am I to say that there is a God? It is the same question. That question doesn't prove anything.

"Some people told me to make AA my higher power. My problem with that is that there were too many humans involved."

The room laughed even harder that time.

"Humanity has had a problem with morals from the beginning of history. I'd always been of the mind that men are corrupt from a very young age. It took me a long time to believe in God. I didn't stay sober until I did. When I first defined God I called it everything I don't know and I don't understand. That way I can learn like it says in a Vision for You. It also said that belief means reliance not defiance. So, I was able to ask myself: how can I defy something that doesn't exist? I defied God, but didn't believe in Him at the same time. How can someone defy something that doesn't exist? It made me realize I wasn't defying God. I was defying others' concepts of God.

"The thing I love about AA is that it is up to me to define my own God. My problem with most organized religions is that they claim too much. A lot of people make the mistake of taking the literal interpretations of their scriptures. Since I've gotten sober I've realized that all religions are true. They all speak to these universal truths about humanity. It is just that people want the literal interpretation of their scriptures because they don't want to do the work of finding out what it really means.

"I don't have a problem with any religious text today. I just have a problem with the way most religions are practiced. I think Christianity has amazing principles. It is just that it isn't practiced too well. This whole planet would be much more peaceful if all any of them did was 'love thy God, and love thy neighbor as thyself.' They're also supposed to love their enemy, but I've never met a Christian that has done that.

"People want everything spelled out for them. Only idiots will take literal interpretations of their texts. I find this problem in recovery as well. It tells us that our literature is only a beginning, but a lot of people in AA won't believe anything outside of the Big Book. They're scared too.

"Some people in AA say that you're not supposed to ask questions. They say 'why' isn't a spiritual question," I said in a sarcastic tone.

"It talks about why in the First Step, the Fifth Step, and the Eleventh Step in the *Twelve Steps and Twelve Traditions*: 'Why must every AA hit bottom first? ...Why must we confess our sins, not just to God and ourselves, but to another human being? ...And why must we meditate and pray?'

"If God is everything and has all the answers, then every question is a spiritual question. I should be able to ask God any question I want. If I don't have an answer, I shouldn't say 'don't ask.' That's not humble. The only thing I should say if I don't have an answer is 'I don't know.' That goes with my definition of God, and 'I don't know' is the only answer that can honestly answer every question. This is why those words are my higher power. 'I don't know' is the first step in learning, and that is what I am on this planet to do.

"Fundamentalism is all about not being able to question things. With fundamentalism, you're supposed to have blind faith. The Big Book talks about the fact that we're not supposed to have blind faith. Fundamentalism leads to a lot of conflict in the world. This is why people blow themselves up and go on rages about who is going to hell. They think it is their call to make the judgement and tell people what is right and wrong and where they are going. They just can't acknowledge that that call is up to God. It is even up to their God, but they don't have the humility to see that they are playing God. This is the problem with fundamentalism, and fundamentalism is about fear. These people need a purpose. To die for a cause is a purpose, and the only sense of self-worth they have ever gotten.

"I think a lot of people get faith and fear confused. It is all over the world. Even in AA. People want certainty, and they don't want to do the research. I don't believe in certainty for this world, for one, and two, I need to ask every question possible. My God wants me to question Him about everything because my God has grown to include everything today, including myself. It was amazing how once I started to believe in something it grew. If I want to know my God, then I need to look inward.

"I need to look inward and relate to all of the people around me because one of the key ways I get to discover myself is by watching and seeing that everyone has the same needs and desires. I think alcoholics take themselves as too unique. Normies drink for the same reason alcoholics do: pleasure. It's just that alcoholics seek that pleasure to insanity, and everyone will seek some type of pleasure in their life to their detriment in one way or another.

"I think everyone in the world struggles with insanity. This is what it talks about in the Big Book when it says 'Pride heads the procession.' Pride tells us we are right about things that are only opinions. We think we're right and the people we disagree with are wrong. This is what leads to all conflict. It is our emotions that bring this about, not reason.

"If anyone is wondering what they are addicted to, it's their emotions. That's what drugs do. They boost pleasure centers in the brain. This is why normal people drink as well. This is also what has fueled my imagination. I couldn't relate to anyone when I got here. Now I realize that I have more in common with people than I ever thought possible. This is proven to me in the way that facial expressions are universal. These universal facial expressions show that everyone has the same emotions. Everyone has roughly the same desires. Everyone has that need for importance, and every human has the same character defects.

"Some people in recovery act like the seven deadly sins were written for alcoholics. They weren't. They were written for mankind as a whole. The literature talks about the seven deadly sins, but those were built into our psyche at creation.

"I hear some people ask the question, 'Even if there is a God, how could he care or do anything for me?' Well my response to that is that there are over 100 billion galaxies in the universe. Each of these galaxies has over 100 billion stars. That is more stars than grains of sand on the earth. It is supposedly only about 4% of the matter we see in this universe. If God can create all of this and keep it in harmony with the way it all functions, then God definitely has the power to care about me and take an active role in my life. I shouldn't put limits on that which has designed everything to function in perfect harmony and symmetry. This has been the Second Step for me, and it has saved my life."

I was done, the room was silent for a couple of seconds and the room responded, "Thanks, Justin."

I was satisfied. In AA people rarely thank someone from the floor, but I got it every time. I got the response that I was looking for.

There were still about ten minutes left for sharing, but after I got out what I wanted to, my eyes went right back to Jessica. I needed her. Just to hold or something—I didn't even know.

The meeting was about over, and the secretary had given me the Promises to read for the end of the meeting.

"Now Justin will read the Promises, and lead us out with a prayer of his choice."

I recited them quickly. Whenever I had something memorized, it just flew right out of my mouth. We all got up in a circle to hold hands and say a prayer so I said, "A moment of silence for the sick and sarcastic both inside and outside of these rooms." Everyone started to laugh, and that is when I said, "God."

Everyone joined in and we all said the Serenity Prayer together, trying to hold in our laughter.

The meeting had just ended, and for some reason Jessica walked to me and asked, "Hey, Justin, that's your name, isn't it?"

"Yup," I replied with an indignant amount of confidence, as though I had never even noticed her before.

"I'm Jessica."

"Great," I said in a nonchalant monotone voice.

I would always give one-word answers to people to try to show them I didn't care about who they were. I said it in this way even though I was nervous.

"That was a funny way to end the meeting. I can't believe that you said that."

"It just comes to me," I said as I smiled.

"Will you walk with me Justin? I'm headed to the bus stop."

"Sure."

"So, how long have you been coming?" I asked.

"I just started coming last month. I have 22 days. I don't know if I like it here, but I don't know what else to do. Both my therapist and my doctor told me that I needed to go if they are going to continue to work with me."

"I've been coming for about 10 years, but I just got two. I like going to meetings. I really don't belong anywhere else," I said as I shrugged my shoulders. "It's another reason I love San Francisco. You can be whoever you want to be here, but sometimes I don't even fit in in this city. Recovery is cool for that. It took me a long time to get sober, but I'm doing good today. I like recovery."

"All this God stuff really gets to me."

"It got to me for a long time too, but I found something I could believe in. Some people in AA are a little too crazy about God—just like I was saying they are scared. You just have to try. You can find something."

"It seems so stupid to me," she said.

"A lot of people don't stay because of it, but my life is so much better. I don't know, I just couldn't do it without AA."

"I'm here because I was told to go or they wouldn't work with me anymore," she said as she looked down.

"Well I sure as hell couldn't have stayed alive without my doctor either. He's the only doctor I've had that has never cussed me out. I've had a lot of doctors scream at me. One was even in charge of a hospital." I wanted to make her laugh, but she didn't respond.

"Can I tell you something about what AA has done for me?" I asked.

"Sure, I mean, what could that be?" She responded.

"It took me a long time to quit drinking and doing drugs, but I never gave up. I always walked back in the next day. People in AA have told me, 'Justin if you can do it, then anyone can.' That is a line of crap. If anyone can do it, then I can do it. So, if anyone can do it, then you can do it. Just don't give up hope, and never stop trying. You should take anything as if it is human, then it can be done by you. Find some type of higher power that will work for you. It doesn't need to be anything that anyone else has. It just needs to make sense to you. Do you hear me?"

"Yeah, but I don't know."

We walked, she talked, and I began to open up a bit. I still didn't let her know I liked her, but she seemed to want to be around me so I was happy inside. I started to tell her all about myself because I usually did that with most people, even strangers.

"You know I should have been dead so many times. I am an epileptic who's bipolar with ADD, dyslexia, obsessive compulsive personality, general anxiety, PTSD, and all the learning characteristics of someone with Asperger's. They say that you shouldn't be terminally unique in AA, but I don't think anyone can argue with me on that one. They say I have aspects of all those disorders, but I don't fit one stereotype completely. Even my seizures are abnormal."

I continued, "I've been on SSDI since 2001, but now I have a part-time job. I'm still on it, but I have a dream of going to school and getting off it someday. I want to make sure you know that there's only one true definition of an asshole."

"What's that?" she responded.

"That is someone who thinks that people wanting to be on disability or any type of government assistance lead a life of luxury. It sucks! They don't let you do anything or have anything. Because of AA, I'm going to get off it. I do entry-level accounting right now. No one ever showed me how. I taught myself. I can't even read too well, but I still do bookkeeping. It has been wonderful to have a purpose. I never had a purpose before AA. I always thought that there wasn't any point to life.

"I am going to make sure I never give up on my dreams and desires. This is what recovery is all about. It is about living life. My life just started. Hell, I was suicidal for most of it—even as a child. That's what I got sent to that boarding school I talked about tonight. My life was nothing but hell, but because of recovery I am enjoying myself. I am having a better life, and it is there for you too."

I told her all of this with a lot of optimism. I wanted to cheer her up. She opened up to me too. She told me that she was on SSDI too.

"What are you on it for?" I asked.

"Chronic fatigue syndrome. I have a hard time functioning in day-to-day life. I've been on it for a while too, and now my doctors want me to go to these stupid meetings."

The 45 bus was coming about a block away, so she asked, "Can I give you my number so you can call me and take me to a meeting or something?"

I was elated inside, so then I asked, "Can you just tell me yours?"

"Don't you need to write it down?"

"No, just tell me. I counted 216 phone numbers in my head one day. I'm sure I can get another. Besides my lack of social skills, I am a savant. There are a couple of reasons that they think I have Asperger's."

She giggled a little, and then told it to me as the bus was coming.

"I'll call you tomorrow, and then we might be able to go to a meeting together!" I said cheerfully.

"I would like that," she replied.

She hopped on, and the bus took off. I felt happy that she was interested in me. I would love to be with someone as adorable as her. I had felt that way before, but I knew that this time it would all work out.

Chapter 3: I Never Back Down

I could have taken the same bus home as Jessica and just walked up the Stockton tunnel stairs on the side of Chinatown, but I thought I would go a different route because I was feeling pretty shy about being around someone that I felt so attracted to.

I was waiting for the 49 bus on the corner of Union and Van Ness. As I was waiting at the stop, all I could do was think of the next time I was going to see her. I had her number in my head. She said she wanted to talk the next day.

The bus came up over the small hill. I looked around to see that there were a couple of people at the stop waiting with me. The bus stopped, and I made sure I was the first person on. It was a pretty empty bus because it was so late at night. I hopped right on and sat down.

There was an elderly black lady getting on behind me who seemed to have a hard time stepping up. After I sat down, the whole bus was still waiting for her to make it up the steps.

When she got to the top of the steps she said to me, "I need that seat. I'm a senior!"

I looked around and saw that besides the old guy sitting right across from me, and a couple of people at the back, the bus was empty. I looked her up and down. She had her hair dyed purple and her face seemed weathered. This town is so weird, I thought; even old people think they are punk rockers.

"There is a seat right there. The whole bus is open, and I have a reason for sitting here."

"You don't have a reason! I'm a senior! I need to sit there! You don't need to sit there! You can stand!" She was continuing to raise her voice at me the whole time.

"Listen, old bitch, it looks like you need a Mohawk with that hairdo! Don't screw with me, Grandma!"

"You shouldn't talk to your elders that way!" She raised her voice even louder.

"I don't respect people just because they've got wrinkles, OK? So shut up and leave me alone. There are plenty of other seats!"

There was this fat old hick sitting across from me who look disturbed. He said to me with a lisp, because he was missing a couple of his front teeth, "Don't talk to a lady that way!" He had a southern twang.

"What the fuck are you gonna do, old man? Knock out a tooth?" I screamed.

"Old man?" he replied.

"That's why you're sitting here, ain't it?"

He sat there in shock with nothing to say.

Then some guy at the back of the bus pointed at me and said, "Hey listen, you little punk, he may not be able to knock out one of your teeth, but I sure as hell can! You know what? Your disability is in your goddamn head!"

That's when I saw that the finger he was pointing at me was missing the tip. It must have gotten cut off or something, so I replied, "Nice finger! Where you born that way, or did your mother cut it off at a young age? And if you hit me you'll be going back to jail! There's a camera right there! You probably should go to jail anyway! I see how you stole those rhinestones that are in your ears! I can tell they're not diamonds by the rest of your attire!" He was dressed in some dirty jeans and an old shirt.

I started to laugh because that was the thing that I always did. I knew in my heart, from all of my experiences, that if you truly want to make someone angry you always have to laugh. Everyone looked shocked and scared.

They all quieted down, and the old black lady hobbled to the back of the bus to get a seat. I could tell that the driver wanted to stay out of it and get home. I spent the rest of the ride chuckling to myself. I played the whole tape in my head about what they said, and what I said. I was laughing out loud to myself, and they could all tell that I was laughing at them.

The rest of the ride was quiet. They were all staring at me, so I put on my headphones and played the music as loud as I could. I was lip syncing "They're Out to Get Me," by my favorite childhood band Guns N' Roses. I could feel their anger, and I knew that I had won. That was all I ever needed to know. It was this high of being able to conquer anyone that made it so I would never back down.

Chapter 4: The View of Another

"She's adorable!" I said to Chris.

Chris was my sponsor in AA. Chris was the first one to take me all the way through the Twelve Steps. No sponsor I ever had took me through the Steps for the first eight years because I couldn't stay sober. Step One is about staying sober in every situation. Every time I relapsed I had to go back to the First Step, but now that I had been sober for two years I finally finished them all.

We were sitting out in front of Macy's where he worked. There is a Peet's Coffee bar outside of Macy's on the side of the building that faces Stockton. I always went to meet him when he was at work. Because I was always going there to see him, I would end up buying a lot of clothes. I was never a clothes whore before, but because of Chris I really started enjoying looking nice.

Chris was always complaining to me about the management and how nothing was ever good enough for them. They would have goals and sales quotas they were all supposed to make, but if they started to get close to their quota, then Macy's would automatically up the goal so no one could get a bonus. They always made each person work harder and harder. Macy's was a corrupt bunch of pricks, but I loved their deals on designer clothes. It was the one place in SF were a person could get Hugo Boss, Zegna, and Michal Kors 50% off. All the other stores in Union Square carried them, but Macy's was the only one would have them on sale. There was always a promotion. It was so ridiculous to think that every week Macy's had the "Biggest One-Day Sale of the Year."

"So, does this mean you're in love with her just from seeing her once?" he asked as he kind of chuckled to himself. "You are such a lesbian, I swear to God. I don't know. I can be the same way. If I have sex with an Asian man, it's all about marriage."

One of his coworkers that worked in the same department, Tommy Hilfiger, came up to the table. Her name was Betsy, and she was the only person at Macy's who never let any of the crap that happened get to her. Betsy walked up to the table as Chris and I were talking and said to him, "I had to ring up one of your sales because you left for lunch, but we can transfer it over once we both get upstairs."

That's when I reached into my pocket and said, "Don't worry, I got this one!" I pulled out a nickel and a couple of pennies and tried to hand it to him while I was smiling.

I was starting to laugh and Chris said, "Watch it, Justin. We all know even she could kick your ass."

He said this because Betsy was a middle aged, four-foot-ten Filipino woman. Chris always told me that I can talk a lot of shit, but that I've never been able to back it up. Chris did his best to let go each one of my insults as though they would never get to him. He kept this really Zen look on his face each time that I was messing with him, but I could tell it got to him sometimes.

"I was just trying to compensate for the .05% commission you guys get here," I said with a grin.

"Do you know that sometimes I can see your mouth moving, but it doesn't seem like anything comes out," Chris said in a peaceful voice.

"Well then maybe I should get you a thicker pair of glasses and a hearing aid, but you probably couldn't make headway with those either," I said smiling even bigger.

I always thought he had on dorky frames. It was weird; Chris was really good at dressing others, but he didn't seem to have any sense of fashion with whatever he wore. He always wore these cheap looking cowboy clothes. It was either Wrangler or some other cheap shirt. I didn't understand because he got even better deals than I did with his discount. They told him he had to wear a tie at work, so all he did was put on one of those cowboy bull ties. I thought that it always looked so terrible, but he liked it.

I could tell I was starting to get to him, so I backed off a little. Chris was one of the people that helped me the most when no one else would. I didn't want to hurt his feelings. I just enjoyed joking with him.

With the last joke, he quickly changed the subject. "Did I tell you about the time that my bandmates and I were cornered in an alley? There were these skinheads that were coming towards us. There was no way out, so I knew that we had to take a stand. I told my bandmates that they would need to cover me and I would take the leader. We beat each one of their asses," Chris said with confidence as he sat up. "It was an amazing fight!"

I always rolled my eyes whenever he went down his tall tale's path. Chris was more of a teddy bear, but he always needed people to think that he was tough. He wasn't. He was about as kind of a person as anyone could ever be. I know this because he never let anything I said ever get to him, and he always showed up for me.

"Oh, shoot! I gotta get back inside. It's been fifteen minutes. Randy's here and he loves to write me up. That man is such an asshole. I wouldn't mind throwing him out the window, but I wouldn't want the pavement to get the pleasure of hitting him first. I need to be the one to do that someday, and no, Justin, I don't think you would learn even from hitting the pavement. You're too ornery. I love and will see you later."

"I love you too. Thanks for the talking. But you know if you hate it so much here, then maybe you can go back to delivering pizzas?"

"The pavement may not teach you anything, but I still might have you try it someday," Chris said with a grin.

"Quick, get back to work! I don't want you getting written up! I won't be able to get good deals on designer clothes if you ever get fired from here."

As Chris went inside there was someone that was approaching people telling them America needed to impeach Obama. These people were always in Union Square trying to convince everyone that Obama was some evil dictator. They would have these pictures of him with Hitler's mustache. I thought it was the sickest thing to compare him to Hitler. They were just crazy white people that were terrified that America was changing. America could elect a black man and they didn't like it.

He came up to me and asked, "Would you like this flier on impeaching President Obama?"

"Wipe your own ass!" I said to him as I got up and walked away. "You inbreeds must love the taste of crap because it's the only thing that ever comes out of your mouths." I raised my middle finger and proceeded to walk away. He just stood there stunned.

I lived up the street above the Stockton Tunnel, so proceeded to walk home. I was just stomping as fast as I could and talking to myself. My mind was busy again, so I was processing more thoughts in a quiet mutter. I just wondered when was the next time I was going to see Jessica. I couldn't wait. I was repeating her number to myself as I was walking up the tunnel.

"When do I get to see you again, Jessica?" I mumbled.

Chapter 5: Give Me a Reason to Stay

After I had gotten back from meeting with Chris at Macy's, I thought I would see if I could get a hold of Jessica. I called her to see if she was going to a meeting that night. She told me she was, so I asked her if I could take her for coffee after the meeting. She said yes, so my hopes were up.

The fact that I would see Jessica had me at the meeting about an hour and a half beforehand. The meeting didn't even start until 8:30 p.m., but I was there at 7:00 p.m. There was this one guy who has been setting up the room for about twenty years from what I heard, and the only thing that I ever heard him say to anyone was "Happy Friday."

It was kind of weird. It seemed as though someone was home, but the only words that ever came out of his mouth were "Happy Friday." He set up the room at about 6:00 p.m., so I knew that the meeting place would be open.

I walked in, and just like clockwork he said, "Happy Friday."

"Happy Friday," I replied in a dull tone. I never knew anything else to say to him.

I had my iPod with me, so I just put on my music and started to lip sync for an hour or so. I was listening to Billy Joel's "Captain Jack." I had only been able to listen to that song recently. It was always one of my favorites, but for the longest time every time I heard that song, I had to go out drinking. It was the best song of all time to get drunk to because it was just how I felt back then.

The theme of the song was your life sucks, but then you drink and everything will be OK. Then your life sucks because you drink, but all you have to do is drink and you'll be taken care of. It was all about the misery of being drunk, and it glorified that misery. When I was drinking, misery was all I had, so I needed that song. I still loved it. Now it was as though I could glorify that misery without the pain of intoxication.

When I was drinking, misery was all there was. I would glorify it when I was out drinking because it was the only thing that gave me comfort. It was the consequence of being so depressed for so long. When I was depressed I would ponder my sorrows and dwell on them. It was trippy because it made it all feel better in a perverse way, but then it would just take me deeper into that insanity.

I used to sing that song as loud as I could, drunk as all hell, just hiking around town. "Captain Jack will get you high tonight, and take you to your special island. Well now, Captain Jack will get you by tonight, just a little push and you'll be smiling." I screamed those words as loud as I could. People were around, but they didn't exist to me. I was on my island with my music. No one could touch me. I was saturated in a glorious depression, and I was completely isolated because my headphones were on. That was the only way I could drink, for oblivion!

I sat there just listening to Billy Joel, playing the air piano, and keeping to the beat of the drums. Then some girl came in and sat down a couple of seats ways from me. It was appalling. She smelled like a cigarette, and I had quit smoking. I had to quit smoking because I developed asthma from all the drugs I did.

I was starting to get really angry just smelling the leftover fumes on her, so I said, "Hey, you smell like a cigarette! Can you sit somewhere else? It's a big room!"

"Relax, babe. I can sit anywhere that I want to. Why don't you move?"

I stood up and I looked her up and down. She was wearing a really tight peach colored skirt with short sleeves. The creases were showing on the side of her dress because it was so tight. It pulled out the pudge in her belly a little.

With that, I put my nose in her face and pointed my finger directly at her and said, "Listen, bitch! The skirt's a little too tight! It's bringing out the wrinkles! Don't... Fucking.... Call me... Babe!" I made sure I was staring at her directly in the eyes, just holding the intensity.

She let out a little "ah" and got up and quickly left the room. I watched her as she sped down the steps.

"Good," I muttered, and as soon as she was completely out of sight I began to laugh.

I sat back down and listened to Billy Joel as more and more people began to come into the room. I didn't need to talk to them. I would just nod my head in hello, and I kept bouncing up and down to the same song.

That's when I saw Jessica walk in. I quickly turned off the music, got up, and walked over to her very quickly.

"How's it going?" I asked.

"Well, I'm here. I have to be."

I stood there looking at her, just wondering what she thought of me. I didn't know. I desperately needed to know what she thought. It was always maddening to contemplate what people were thinking of me, but that's where my mind would always go. With her I really wanted to figure it out, but all I could do was just stand there in a nervous wonder.

"Do you want to sit next to me?" I asked. "I'm right here in the front."

"I can't sit in the front. I don't want all the people noticing me. It's too much. I can't sit in the front."

I could never go to a meeting without sharing. I always had to sit in the front, so I said, "OK, well I'll be here, and after the meeting we can go for a cup of coffee. Is that OK? I wonder who is speaking tonight." I looked all around. "Oh God! Not her! This bitch is so crazy. I don't know if I can sit through her share again."

This lady I had heard a million times was sitting down at the table. I could tell she was the one speaking, and it annoyed me because she was always so corny and melodramatic. She wanted to dramatize each and every word that came out of her mouth. Some people in these rooms think that they are so profound, and she was one of them. I was thinking of leaving, but I wanted to be with Jessica. I was really looking forward to after the meeting, so I just took a seat.

"I'm going to go sit in the back. We'll get together after the meeting, right?"

"Yes, we will," I responded.

The next hour all I heard was blah, blah, blah... I heard this old ho' say something like, "working the Steps right was like having sex. If you do it with someone you love and care about it can be amazing."

She always used that analogy to try and get people to laugh, but the problem is that I had heard her say it a million times. I thought it was stupid enough the first time. This old prude thought she was so clever for saying it too.

After she was done sharing, she picked the topic of: fellowship, and we can't do this alone. I was the only one that had my hand raised in the room, so she called on me.

"Thank you for that analogy about sex. It was really profound," I said with a slight amount of sarcasm. "Each night I pray to the ancient god Dionysus. He is the god of wine, fertility, and drunken orgies."

Some of the room started to laugh.

"I really appreciate your analogy, and I have some friends that are crystal addicts. They all have one requirement every time that they go to hook up with someone. They can't know the person's name, so your concept about it being better with someone you love and care about is right on." I said this with an intense amount concern and caring.

She could tell that I was being sarcastic. She was getting this disgusted look on her face, but everyone else was laughing.

I continued, "When it comes to fellowship, you're right, I can't do this alone. Before I got to AA I was never told to come back anywhere. Even in AA there were people that couldn't stand me, but they all told me to keep coming back. That was the only thing that worked for me for a long time. In the Big Book, it talks about how when we were drunk we sought out lower companions. When I was drunk there were no lower companions. I was too hostile and difficult.

"Every time I got drank for the first year I was in San Francisco I blacked out. I might get arrested, get in a fight, and wake up strapped down to a gurney in San Francisco General Hospital three nights a week. I never won one of those fights either. I would always get my ass kicked. I couldn't even quit drinking on Antabuse. When I got into speed I would spend hours looking for more. Speed is a crazy drug, and it is the worst for me because I'm an epileptic.

"Speed causes more seizures than anything else. The problem was that the medications they give you for epilepsy counteract the high. The medications block the chemicals in your brain from going up, and speed tries to boost them. Because of this I would stop taking my medication, and then I would have large seizures and wake up in the hospital.

"When I did speed, I smoked everything on the ground: kitty litter, dirt, and wax." All of this was true, except for praying to Dionysus. "I was crazy, and I couldn't get along with anyone, but people in AA were willing to love me until I could love myself. This was the only thing that ever worked. I tried a lot of people's patience in these rooms too. I got an arson charge in an AA meeting one night. One time I was at a meeting and I pissed on someone's motorcycle, then I held his hand during the closing prayer as I told him."

More people started to laugh.

I finished with, "It is all because of AA that I've been able to get sober and get somewhat acclimated into society. I didn't belong anywhere. I'm sober, and I love my life today. I have a good job and I'm happy. I also don't do a lot of the crazy stuff that I used to do. I don't get in fights every night anymore. None of that stuff happens anymore. All I'm saying is I'm grateful for the fellowship. Without AA, I wouldn't be alive."

I was silent for a little while, and everyone in the room was trying not to laugh too hard. The speaker looked disgusted. I didn't care. I wanted her to hate me. She was one of those idiots I had heard one too many times.

The room still responded with, "Thanks, Justin."

Some more people shared, and when the meeting only had about five minutes left, the secretary said, "Now it's time for a burning desire. A burning desire is if someone who needs to share because they feel as though they might drink, harm themselves, or someone else."

"I feel like harming someone else," I shouted out with a big smile on my face staring right at the speaker. I wanted her to know I couldn't stand her.

Everyone started to laugh and the secretary said, "Thanks, Justin" in a dull tone.

We all closed with the Serenity Prayer. Then I went up to Jessica and asked, "Do you want to get out of here?"

"Give me a minute. I need to get a signature from the secretary to show my doctor and my therapist."

"It's cool."

I followed her to the front of the room and saw her pull out a slip with a whole bunch of signatures on it. It was weird. I looked at her hands. Her hands looked like an old witch's hands. They weren't long, but they definitely looked skinny and bony. She had a very young vibrant face. Her face was gorgeous, but her hands looked withered and wrinkled. You could see the veins poking out of them. It kind of gave me a creepy feeling. I didn't know why, but it confused me more than anything.

I was walking out of the room with Jessica and I heard this guy Seth ask another guy, Brian, "Hey, can you give me a ride home? I live in the Presidio, and I know you live out that way. Jerry said he would, but I don't want to have him go so far out of his way. I'll pay you back."

Seth was a really big macho straight guy, so I said in a nonchalant way as I was walking out the door, "Just give him a blow job."

I made sure that they saw me laughing to myself. I could feel Seth's eyes burning into the back of my head.

We walked down the front steps and out of the building, through the brick courtyard where everyone was smoking. I was thinking she might be older than I thought, so I asked in kind of a nervous inquisitiveness, "So how old are you?"

"I'm getting old. I just turned forty-two this year. Can you slow down? I'm in a little pain. I have some fibroid cysts on my ovaries, and it hurts when I walk too fast. I just got on some birth control for them, and my doctor said that it will take a couple of weeks for them to shrink."

I was shocked! She looked so young. I couldn't believe it. How can someone look like they're in their twenties when they are forty-two? I didn't care. She was so beautiful, and my mother and father were about ten years apart. I truly didn't mind. If she was going to be the one for me, then I knew it would work out.

We were walking slowly up to the coffee shop on Union and Fillmore. It wasn't a great place. It was always cold inside, but there was no other place to go. It was only a block away from the meeting, but we could be alone there because everyone else goes to fellowship somewhere else.

"So how are you liking the meetings so far?" I asked.

"Nothing too special. I just really came to see you. I mean I have to get the slip signed, but I would rather get to know you than come to these meetings."

I felt happy. Wonderful, I thought.

She proceeded, "I've gotten a sponsor, and am working the steps just like I've been told to do, but my sponsor is too crazy. Most people here are. My sponsor told me that she would work with me, but she also told me she always gets resentments against good-looking women. She said that she always takes attractive women as competition. She told me that she needs to be the best looking. She was still willing to work with me because that is the only way that she can stay sober. She seems so crazy."

"A lot of people that stay sober are still pretty crazy," I said. "Hell, I think everyone is, everyone in the world, not just alcoholics. If all it takes to be insane is doing the same thing over and expecting a different result, well everyone does that. They have to because all they have to deal with in the present moment is their past experiences. The only thing that someone can do is something that worked for them in the past. When people don't know what to do next, they just do what worked for them at one time in their life; so everyone is crazy, according to Albert Einstein. Just look at the world.

"I mean think about it, most people in AA believe that they are so unique. It is true what they say about alcoholics needing to take themselves as terminally unique. I did for a long time, but now I explain most things in paradoxes. Yes, I am unique, but everyone is. Yet we are all made of the same chemicals, we all have the same emotions, motivations, and all our desires are basically the same.

"I put every person in the world on some type of numerical scale between one and zero. If you think about it there is an infinite amount of number between one and zero. They're close together, relatively speaking, but you can always divide one by any other number. So, there is an infinite amount of irrational numbers between one and zero. I'm not saying that the numbers mean anything except that each person is unique, and we're all a lot closer than we think.

"Everyone wants some type of accomplishment. I do too. A lot of people in recovery are still pretty crazy, but they are also some of the best people that I've ever met. The happiest people are the ones that work a good program, from what I've seen. I'm also a lot happier than I've ever been. I no longer want to die. Death was something that I focused on throughout my childhood and young adult life. I enjoy life today."

I would always catch myself rambling really fast and talking about stuff that was too intellectual for most people, so I just tried to shut up.

"Talk about suicidal. My Fourth Step makes me feel like dying. I don't like bringing up all this stuff. I feel as though I should just let go," she said, moping. "So how long have you been coming?"

"Since July of '98. I came in because of my epilepsy. My doctor told me if I didn't quit drinking, I would have brain surgery or die. It was the fear of death that got me into AA, but it never kept me sober. I tried for a long time, but I guess it's just that I never gave up. That's why I'm sober, and that's why I'm happy. I can't even count how many times I've tried killing myself. Look at my neck. I have a scar from trying to cut my throat, but I'm pretty happy today."

I put my hand against my neck and pulled up the skin to show her the razor mark.

You can be happy too. The reason why I show it to people is to let them know they can get through it."

"I've been through a lot myself. I've lost my family. My father died of brain cancer, and my mother died of breast cancer. I'm an only child, so I really don't have anyone. I live with a guy, Theo; he's kinda like family. It's crazy, though; his family is so perfect it makes me sick. They're like *Leave it to Beaver*. His family doesn't like me much. They think that I'm making his life worse. How about you; what's with your family?"

"I got shipped away to a boarding school for behavioral problems when I was young. After that, I got kicked out of the house because I was having seizures undiagnosed, and my mom wanted me to drive a car and get a job. I told her no because I was losing my consciousness three times a day, but she told me I had to get out, so I moved down here with my uncle. I love SF. I don't belong anywhere else. I'm too awkward to be anywhere else," I said.

We got to the coffee shop, and I got a green tea. I couldn't drink coffee anymore because of all the drugs I did, so I just got a green tea. She got an iced latte with extra ice. I really didn't understand extra ice.

Then she asked me, "Are you seeing anyone?"

I felt really happy because it seemed as though she was interested in me. "No," I replied with a nervous anticipation. "I've always wanted to be with someone, but right now I'm single. I was in a relationship with this crazy girl until recently. We broke up because she was doing a lot of shady stuff. I couldn't be around her anymore." I realized that I was giving too much information again so I shut up again.

"Like what?"

"Just lying and stealing. She was sober, but she just really didn't work a program. I took her as a narcissist with a drug-induced psychosis. Her doctors said she's bipolar, but she's not. There's all different types of crazy, but she takes the cake."

"Yes, but what did she do?"

"I don't really want to get into it. How about you? Are you seeing anyone?"

"I'm kind of seeing someone, but he lives in New York. I don't really want to go see him. I have a trip planed in a couple of days, but would you be able to give me some reason to stay here?"

I was shocked. I didn't know what to think. She was saying she wanted me, but she also just told me that she was with someone. I don't like invading another person's relationship. That would be dishonest. I couldn't do that. I didn't want to be the reason she would break up with someone, nor did I want to feel responsible for this guy's hurt feelings.

She continued, "My roommate Theo thinks he is a terrible person. He is abusive in a lot of ways. He would always insult me. One time he even told me that I was a sociopath. It was really hurtful. I don't know why I'm with him, but would you give me a reason to stay? Just give me a reason not to visit him. I would really like that."

"Uh, I don't know." I didn't know what to think or do.

As all of this was going on, I started to feel one of my seizures coming on. I was starting to have a seizure, so I said to her, "Watch my eyes."

"Why, what's going on?"

"I'm having a seizure; just watch my eyes. The pupils get really small; then, just watch them, they will dilate; then they'll start to oscillate back and forth."

"You're having a seizure!" She said this with a frightening tension in her voice. She was staring to panic.

"Don't worry about it," I responded, "I have them every day. There are lots of different types of seizures. Most people think there is only one kind—when someone is flopping around on the ground. I just have simple, partial, and partial complex. Simple means I don't lose my consciousness, and the complex means I do. I haven't had too many complex ones since I got sober this last time. I mostly have a lot of the simple ones every day. They're nothing to worry about. They're harmless. I can get kind of manic sometimes because of them, but they're not dangerous."

"Oh, well, why does it make you manic?"

"Every time I have a seizure the chemicals in my brain fluctuate. That means that the dopamine can go either up or down in my brain. When I have a lot of them, I get hypomanic. It's not bad, just a little excited. It actually feels pretty good—kinda like I'm on a little bit of speed," I said with a smile.

"What causes them?"

"I have what's called a heterotopic gray matter. It's a nerve that everyone has had from early womb to early childhood development. It's kind of like an appendix. No one knows its purpose, but it's what sends the electronic signals that cause my seizures. That's what a seizure is. It's an electronic disturbance in the brain." I was used to explaining this to everyone. "Everyone has gray matter on the outside of their brain. I just have some adjacent to my right lateral ventricle and my right frontal horn. It is also what is speculated to cause my bipolar disorder."

"You know a lot about it."

"All I do is listen. I'm amazed by the number of people that don't know anything about their own medical conditions. Most people just trust their doctors, but I've seen too many doctors that have no clue on what they are doing. I have two good ones now. They are the best two that I've ever seen. My psychiatrist, Richard Shapiro, is the only psychiatrist I've had that's never cussed me out. Paul Garcia is an extremely intelligent neurologist. He was the one to diagnose me."

There was a bit of silence, and then she spoke up again, "So, will you give me a reason not to go? I would really like that. Please give me a reason."

Then I looked at my watch. "Damn! I have to get going. I get up at six on the weekends to go to the 8:00 a.m. meeting. It's already 10:00. Maybe I will see you at the Grace Cathedral meeting on Wednesday at 6:00 p.m."

"That's right near my apartment. I live in Chinatown. I just have to walk up a couple of blocks. But will you give me reason not to go on that trip? He's not a good person, and I want to be with a good person. Can you give me a reason?"

"I'll see you Wednesday night. I have to get going," I said as I started to walk out of the coffee shop.

I couldn't get in the middle of a relationship. I'm not like that. I don't lie and I don't cheat. "I just can't," I mumbled, walking out the door.

I thought I would get home as fast as I could so I could get up and go to the 8:00 a.m. meeting. I was blue, lonely, and I just wanted someone to be with. What I wanted was to be with Jessica, but I couldn't steal someone away from another person.

Chapter 6: The Saints, Brahman, and Darwin

The group that an AA member chooses to go to on a regular weekly basis is their home group. I was asked to speak at my home group, the 7 a.m., where I go every weekday. The Wednesday morning meeting is a step study, and we were on the Third Step: "Made a decision to turn our will and our lives over to the care of God as we understand him." I got up at 5 a.m. to make sure I was there early.

My concept of a higher power was pieced together from a lot of different belief systems. I would listen to what people said about God, both inside and outside of AA, and come to my own conclusion. Some of what people believe made sense to me, but I also thought that no one could be completely right. It was like a puzzle that I put together on my own. It was a puzzle that was made by me and for me.

A lot of people in AA spent a lot of time with the anti-intellectual argument for God, which disgusted me. I would always hear people say, "figuring out is not a slogan." As though I was just supposed to have blind faith. The Big Book has a section which tells us that blind faith isn't the way to go, but a lot of people choose that route because they don't have the answers. Some people really like what I had to say, but there were also those who thought I wanted to analyze everything too much. I knew this morning I had to speak out against blind faith. Blind faith causes too many problems in this world.

I got to the meeting and I had already known what I was going to talk about in my share. It would never take me long to plan to say anything, but if there was the topic to talk about beforehand I would always have something ready.

We went through all the readings as I was sitting in my spot. The same spot that I always sat in: the first chair to the left of the secretary. "I have asked Justin to share his experience with Step Three this morning," the secretary said.

"My name is Justin, and I'm an alcoholic."

"Hi Justin," the whole room responded.

"Saint Anselm said it best; if one is doubting or can't believe in God: 'Take a chance on the truth instead of living your life in error.' If God doesn't exist, then it truly doesn't matter what anyone believes in. If all humans are a bleep in time, with no purpose behind any of it, then nothing is meant to truly matter in the long run. Everyone lives by faith, whether they choose to believe it or not. How many people here believe that Mt. Everest is the tallest mountain in the world? How many of you have been to Mt. Everest and measured it? How many of you have measured Mt. Everest and then measured every other mountain in the world? You believe it is the tallest mountain all because someone told you, and it fits with your experiences. This is the same reason that people think that Jesus is the son of God.

"People take a lot of what they see and hear as true for this very reason, but people are often led astray by their mind, which is meant for nothing but the purpose of interpreting what they perceive. This tells me that faith is something which is built within us from the beginning. Faith is about belief, nothing more.

"People believe all kinds of things, and a lot of their beliefs contradict what others believe. Each one says to the other they are right and the others are wrong. If it's about God, politics, or what anyone chooses to take as important, everyone believes that their beliefs are true. A lot of people that are from the same religions will have different interpretations of their literature as well. When they're asked to explain the same belief system they can come up with different ways of understanding and explaining the same text. No two minds are completely alike; so, all truth is based on the individual. This is what is meant when they say truth is relative, or relativity. So yes, truth is relative; so, absolute knowledge can't be achieved by anyone human.

"People are always quoting Albert Einstein in recovery, but there are problems with his theories too. Even though they are the best ways for describing certain things, they can't explain others. What I take as true and perfect I choose to call God, and my main reasons for coming to this belief is the Catholic saints. Anselm, Aquinas, and Augustine give wonderful explanations for the existence of God and why He works the way He does. To me, it's not so much about Christ as it is just about something existing that is the main cause and has all the answers.

"I'm a human, so my mind will always have limits. I am constantly looking and exploring what a higher power is and what it means to me. I take my higher power as the ultimate reality. I can only see this ultimate reality once I can get past my mind. My mind has led me to the doorway, but it can only take me so far. I need to have faith. This faith has shown me that God is everything today, including myself. I am just a piece of God. We all are, yet for the people that question faith, their main argument against there being a God seems to be: Why is there such a thing as evil with a perfect being?

"Augustine justifies this evil by saying that life is about learning. The problem of evil in the world keeps lots of people from being willing to believe in God. A lot of people who come to recovery refuse to believe in God because of the hand that they were dealt in life. Augustine tells how pain is the only way a human, and any life for that matter, can learn and grow. So, life is about learning. The need to learn is within all of us. There are people in recovery who say that if there was a God, then why wouldn't It make us all perfect too. They say there is too much suffering in life.

"It is a paradox because the reason no one will ever be perfect is because we need to continue to learn, but we learn that we can be perfect if we have God in our lives. We're just a piece of Him. We all are, and if God is everything, then we are incomplete without each other. This is why we will always need to continue to learn.

Life is about learning—not just to Augustine, but to Aquinas as well. Aquinas' main proof for God is that all life has intelligence. This intelligence shows that there is a reason to life. This reason is God. Without God, how could anything have the will to continue to learn? Learning is my secret to life.

"I have found my purpose in the lessons of life. I feel as though I can be grateful for all that I go through in this day. As long as what I experience is a chance to grow and learn, then everything I go through has a purpose. I take God as the ultimate teacher. This ultimate teacher has all the answers shows us all how it works.

"In Hinduism, the Godhead is the Brahman. The Brahman is beyond infinity. The Brahman includes all. What we truly are is the Atman. Everyone has an Atman. The Atman is like a spirt that is in each one of us, and it is the only thing that we truly are. Our bodies, minds, and perceptions are illusory substances. The goal for every Atman is to be united with the Brahman. The only way that I might be able to have any insight into the Brahman is to explore my own Atman.

"There is a line I completely disagree with in the Big Book and that line is: 'Self-knowledge avails us nothing.' The self is the only thing I can truly know, so I look inward, and it is not just me. Ibn al-Arabi, the greatest Sufi mystic of all time said, 'Whoever knows himself, knows his Lord.' This tells me the only place I need to look is inward to find all my answers because that is where God is.

"The paradox continues with the fact that one of the best ways for me to look inward is to relate myself to the outside world. If I am just a piece of God, then I need to relate myself to the other pieces of Him around me. To find what I have in common with others makes me learn more about myself. I use the stimulation of the outside world to continue to grow into a better person. I use this stimulation to develop my mind. Once I have the answers it is because I have gotten past my mind into the Atman.

"Another amazing thing is that we all are the same. Each person's Atman is identical with the others. This is because the Atman and the Brahman are one. This means that all the differences we judge each other by are all superficial. Our perceptions of this world are unique, but when we get to our true self, we aren't. The true self is identical for everyone because the true self is nothing but the consciousness that we all have. The one thing that is identical to everyone that we all have is our consciousness. I got this from a speech I heard once and it sounded good to me. I heard this guy Jeff say that the images we have of ourselves are always less than our true selves because it is in our true selves where we find God.

"All the answers are beyond the human mind. Knowing I don't have all the answers makes me strive for more, so I strive for perfection through learning, and the only true satisfaction is that I will always fall short. I will always have more to learn so long as I am in this body, and God will always have more to teach me and everyone. Learning isn't just in religion, but it is in science as well.

"Darwin's theory of natural selection is about learning. Darwin says that evolution is about life's natural desire to strive for perfection. Life will never get to be perfect, but this innate desire keeps us evolving for the better. With natural selection, any life that loses its ability to learn and adapt becomes extinct. This also supports Aquinas; so, with Darwin, Augustine, and Aquinas, life is about learning. This is what it is about for me too.

"Even in Hinduism, life is about learning because of karma. Karma is something that each of us gives to ourselves with the way we live our lives. When we take the wrong action, we need to be taught the lesson, and when we take the right action we are awarded with serenity and happiness. The consequences of our actions are about learning; so with karma, life is about learning.

"The word karma in Sanskrit just means action, and these actions that we take go very well with a Newtonian law. Newton discovered that every action that is in the universe is followed by an opposite and equal reaction. This tells me that when I do something wrong, I am not just punishing another, but I am also punishing myself. When I harm someone, I am taking that negative energy out on another and it comes right back to me. This is karma.

"Life being about learning means that to me reincarnation would be God's only viable option. If there is a God, which has been shown to me though my experience, and the Atman is eternal, then reincarnation would have to be. There is too much to learn in one lifetime. My mind is limited to my eyes that were given to me at birth. I would need another life with a different pair of eyes to be able to see anything differently than what I am meant to see in this lifetime. This journey has just begun for me, and since the lessons of life are endless for all, they have just begun for everyone.

"No matter how many lifetimes I have, God would always be loving enough to want to teach me more about Himself until I am united with Him. So, it is with the saints and all other spiritual beings that I get to explore my path. I have found that God is loving enough to build in me the desire to grow. The best teachers always teach the subject until the pupil learns. I was saying that everyone needs faith in order to understand what is out there in the world. This world is too difficult to comprehend completely, and because I need faith, that faith was built into me at birth.

"Faith is something that we all need to get to our higher power, so it is this higher power that installed it in all of us to begin with. This higher power is the Atman because the Atman and the Brahman are one. This is my main reason for believing in God. God knows I can't see Him without faith, and this is why it was built into me from the beginning of creation. I have taken a chance, and that chance has led me to God, so it is with God that I have a reason for what I go through, and that is I will always, in every lifetime, continue to grow and learn. This is what the loving teacher is all about.

"Some people in recovery deny this premise of learning. Some say 'figure it out is not a slogan.' To me, 'figure it out' is the only slogan. It is shown this all throughout the steps. First, I have to figure out I am an alcoholic; then I have to figure out I am powerless over alcohol; then I have to figure out what my higher power is; then I have to figure out how to surrender to my higher power; then I have to figure out what my resentments are; then I have to figure out what my part in those resentments are; then I have to figure out if I can find someone that I trust to reveal all of those defects about myself to; then I have to figure out what my shortcomings are; then I have to figure out how to turn those shortcomings over so I can get them removed; then I have to figure out who on my resentments list I have to make amends to; then I have to figure out who I can and cannot make that amends to, and the best way to do that without hurting those people or anyone else; then I have to figure out how to do all of these steps on a daily basis; then I have to figure out the best way to meditate and pray on a daily basis, and the rewards and awareness that come with that; then I have to figure out how to take everything that I have learned, practice it on a daily basis, and carry that message to the next alcoholic; because that is the only way that I get to stay sober and be happy. I need to teach it to another alcoholic and carry that message to each and every person that comes across my path with the way I live my life. This is what the Twelve Steps mean to me.

"'Figure it out' is the only slogan that means anything. People that tell you ' don't have the answers,' they don't like the fact that they don't have the answers. They choose that slogan because they can't figure it out. They just don't realize that we're not supposed to figure it out, but we are always supposed to try. This world is littered with paradoxes. We can never give up trying to figure it out, and it will always lead us back to the point where we do not know. To admit that you don't know is the answer because 'I don't know' is where it all begins. 'I don't know' is the only answer that will honestly answer any question about this physical world. It's just about an open mind. Thank you."

Everyone clapped because that is what they always do no matter who shares in a meeting. I heard a lot of people respond. Some of them really liked it, but most of them got offended with me bringing up outside philosophies and religions. It would always make me so angry when I would hear people try to deny logic or some other type of solution. I have always objected to the average way most people think. I liked thinking outside the box, and the problem with people in recovery is they can't. They just won't, but I had a purpose of shining light on things. Even if they didn't like it, I knew I had to.

Only some of the people shared on the topic. A lot of them just talked about something else, or shared in a way to prove me wrong.

The meeting was coming to an end, so they read a Vision for You. Then the secretary said, "Now Justin will lead us out with a prayer of his choice."

We all got up to hold hands. I wanted to make those people who objected to what I said feel stupid. Each person there always talked about an open mind. Some of them have an open mind, but a lot of them are just as closed minded as the religions that they grew up with—the religions that they condemned for their narrow mindedness. If a belief doesn't fit with their own, then they just reject it. The Big Book tells us not to do that, but most of them don't care.

We were all holding hands so I said, "A moment of silence for all of those who still resent Christ." I said that because a lot of people were angry that I talked about the Catholic saints and other religions. A lot of people that go to AA, especially gay AA, which this meeting was, have a problem with Christianity. They had a problem with me talking about the saints, and I had a problem with their narrow mindedness.

Once I said this they were all looking around at each other asking each other, "Huh? What?" They all looked confused.

So, I said, "Our Father."

Usually when people close with the Lord's Prayer in an AA meeting there are lots of people that refuse to join in, but they all looked frightened that I saw their resentment. They all knew I was speaking to their closed mindedness. They were all looking around at each other in shock. There wasn't one person that didn't join in on the prayer. This lady Lorain and this other guy Joe were the only ones that were laughing. Everyone else seemed frightened and nervous, but they all joined in.

I kept a straight face and was looking around the room into each one of their eyes. I was reciting with a sincere look on my face and a grin in my heart. I was laughing to myself all throughout the whole prayer in my head.

When the meeting was over, no one wanted to talk to me. I won! I was holding my head high and giggling as I walked out of the meeting. If they were all so open minded, then they could use anyone's words to surrender to their God. That's all I do. I'm not Catholic, Hindu, or a Muslim. I'm not even a scientist, but I do believe in what people have told me about the saints, Brahman, Darwin, and the scientific method.

Chapter 7: We Skip a Meeting Together

Jessica called and asked me if we could meet Wednesday night to get together with her. On Wednesday nights at the church called Grace Cathedral, there was another meeting I was going to. The meeting was at 6 p.m., and she lived close to it. She lived on the edge of Chinatown, and Grace Cathedral was right above Chinatown on the top of a very steep hill, which is called Nob Hill.

Jessica told me to meet her at a coffee shop on the edge of Chinatown. I walked up Stockton to California Street. Then I took a left up a really steep hill all the way to Grace Cathedral. Jones Street was the street that was right in front of Grace Cathedral. I walked down Jones until I got to the coffee shop. I wanted to see Jessica. I wanted to see her even though I didn't think that we would ever be together.

As I was approaching the coffee shop there was a cable car that was speeding by. I saw the cable car coming, so I walked out in front of it really slowly. I did it just to throw the driver off. I could tell the pace I needed to walk to keep from getting hit. I wanted to frighten all the tourists that were taking the car headed down to Fisherman's Warf. They were in shock, and they all saw me with a big smile on my face.

I held my middle finger in the air. I was holding it right up to the driver. The driver yelled at me, "Get out of the way!"

As I stepped on the other side of the tracks, the cable car sped right behind me. I looked back and the cable car was stalled in the middle of the road. I saw that it was going to take him a little time to get it running again. I was chuckling to myself as I walked into the coffee shop.

Jessica was sitting right in the front. She wasn't looking out the window so she didn't see what I just did.

"I'm not going to New York to see him" were the first words that came out of her mouth.

"OK."

"Can I ask you a favor?" She asked in a soft tone.

"Sure." I was nervous, but it came out as confident. I didn't know what she would ask, but I knew I couldn't say no. Does this mean she broke up with him? My mind was racing. I wanted to get to know her, and even see if she could be my girlfriend — especially if she wasn't going to be with that guy.

"Would you mind coming back to my place, and we could skip this meeting together? I'll show you where I live. It is right down the street."

"That would be cool!" I said with a smile as I almost shouted.

I didn't know what else to think except that I was happy she wasn't going to New York. This wasn't on me now. I wasn't stealing her away from her boyfriend. I felt better about seeing her. She didn't want him anymore, and I didn't get in the middle of the relationship. I felt good, but at the same time a little nervous. I also didn't know what we were going to do next at her apartment. I was eager.

"Let me show you where I live. It is over on Jackson Street. We just have to walk a block and a half. Do you know where Jackson Street is?"

"Yes. We're on Sacramento right now. It is just a block north. Is it off Jones?"

"Yes."

"OK, so it is right over there," I said as I pointed north.

As we were walking, she said to me, "I'm not going to New York to see David. He's just an abusive man. I just broke up with him because of it. I would really like to get to know you. I feel as though we have a connection. I told you I wanted a reason to stay, and I found that reason."

I was walking and listening. I didn't respond. I was just happy that she liked me. I couldn't show her how I felt about her yet.

We walked over to Jackson Street and then took a right down the hill. Her apartment in was in one of the old Victorian houses. It looked a little grungy on the outside, but all of these houses looked grungy.

The paint was old and peeling off, and there wasn't any room between the buildings. The paint was a faded blue. The house had a black metal gate out front. The gate had been painted over with some black lacquer about a hundred times. It had peeled with the wear and tear the weather had brought upon it.

As we walked into the apartment, there were these steep steps we had to walk up. The carpet was gray with splotches all over it. It looked as though it hadn't been washed in about twenty years. The walls had been designed out of wood and had been carved out quite well, but they were old too. This whole place looked pretty beat up. I thought it was more of a dump, but as we got to the top of the steps, the apartment looked spacious inside. I mean the hallways were narrow, but there were a lot of different rooms.

There was a living room in the front. Right next to the living room there was one bedroom. At the very top of the stairs, there was another bedroom, and then Jessica had her bedroom as well. They had three bedrooms, two bathrooms, and a kitchen.

We both took a left at the top of the stairs and walked toward the kitchen. Jessica's room was to the right of the kitchen.

"You have a three-bedroom apartment in San Francisco! How can you afford that? This town is so expensive! I'm paying one thousand fifty for a studio."

"My two roommates and I, Theo and Rob, we've been here for about twenty years. The reason why this place is in bad condition is that it is so cheap, and we don't want to piss off the landlords. We only pay nine hundred a month, so we don't complain at all."

"Nine hundred! That's amazing! I wouldn't give my landlord a hard time either."

We walked into her room, and there were pictures everywhere. The pictures were mainly of one lady. It looked like some type of old movie star. It was a white lady with blond hair and bright red lipstick. She had a very beautiful face. The only picture of anyone else was a very sexy picture of Jessica on the wall in lingerie.

Jessica looked amazing. In this picture, she was in nothing but a bra and a thong. She did have very large breasts, especially for such a short woman, and they were hanging right out of the bra. Her hair was combed over to one side, and she was bent over looking directly into the camera. She was on her elbows lying on a bed. She was staring anyone down who looked at the picture. You could see her perfect ass bending up above her back. It was amazing to see the amount of cool confidence Jessica had in that picture.

"I know it might seem like I'm a narcissist with that picture," she said in a soft voice, "but it won a lot of awards when I was in art college. That's the only reason it is up on the wall."

"Cool! You're an artist? My brother was an artist. He almost had a full scholarship to Pratt in New York. Have you heard of Pratt?"

"Every artist has heard of Pratt. You talk about him in the past tense. What happened to him?"

"My brother was a paranoid schizophrenic. When they put him on his medication he couldn't draw or paint. It killed all his artistic ability. He had the worst case of schizophrenia that I ever saw. He thought all the carbon monoxide in the air was making him hallucinate, so whenever he went around a car or went downtown, he had to wear a big World War II gas mask. He got a lot of weird looks. He ended up shooting himself. I don't blame him. He was miserable, and the medication took his life away from him. It was like the movie *A Beautiful Mind*. You know the one about John Nash."

"I heard of that one, but I never saw it."

"Well, in the movie, the medications that they put John Nash on kill all of his intelligence. The same thing happened to my brother. It was sad. No one wants to live like that. He was the most talented artist that I had ever met. Who is this lady that is on the wall? She looks like a movie star of some kind."

"It is Grace Kelly. She was the most beautiful person that I have ever seen. No one else in the world had ever had a face as perfect as her. I'm in love with her. I wish I could have met her. She was so beautiful. I'm always re-watching the movies that she starred in. Alfred Hitchcock used her a lot, and I love all the Hitchcock movies. It's terrible how he never got an Academy Award. That is one of the worst crimes in all of movie history. Hitchcock was one of the best directors of all time, and he took the movie industry in a new direction. They're going to be playing *Vertigo* at the Castro Theater soon if you want to see it with me. Would you be willing to go with me? Theo is going to be coming too. I think it is the best movie of all time. It is my favorite."

"Cool. I'll go. I've never see a Hitchcock movie. I don't go to the movies too often, but I enjoy a good movie."

She went over and sat down on her bed. She had a queen bed, and the blankets looked as old as everything else in the apartment. "Come here. Sit with me," she whispered.

She seemed so confident and daring, so I complied. I went over to sit down on the bed. As I did, she patted my leg and said to me, "I'm glad I didn't go. I want to get to know you. Come here. Come a little closer." With that, she leaned over and gave me a kiss on the cheek. It was all so fast and sudden. It was also what I wanted.

"I'm grateful you didn't go either. I really want to get to know you. I feel a way about you that I haven't felt in a long time."

It wasn't true because I had just gotten out of a relationship, but it sure as hell felt like a long time, and it seemed like the right thing to say. I was starting to get aroused because she was so close to me. I was sitting on her bed, just staring at her big brown eyes. I was in love with them, and she had just given me a kiss on the cheek, so I leaned in and gave her a little peck on the lips.

"Thank you," she whispered. "I needed that. I needed that from someone I know I can trust."

"I'm the most trustworthy person there is. I had someone tell me once that I am constitutionally incapable of not telling the truth." I laughed a little, but it was an awkward thing to say right then, and she didn't even respond to it. So, I was cussing myself out in my head because what I said was so stupid. "Does this mean you're my girl?" I asked.

"I would love to be. That's why I'm staying here. I could tell you wanted me, and I want you. Thank you for the kiss. Come here and just lay down with me."

She leaned back on the pillows and pulled me over to her. I was so turned on, but I knew I had to be a gentleman. I couldn't take it as far as I wanted to go. We were lying there for a while. She was up on the pillows, and I had my head on her chest.

My head was lying right on her right breast. I had arrived. I was in heaven. I felt complete. This is what I wanted. I wanted love. That had been all I ever wanted. It felt amazing, as we were lying there for I don't know how long. Neither of us said much.

Then I heard the front door open. The steps were so old that I could hear them squeaking as someone was walking up. "That must be Theo," she said.

It was already about 6:30, and the footsteps were getting louder and louder, as I could tell he was walking toward her room. I was feeling a little sad that I would have to take my head off her chest to meet him. I didn't want to do anything except lie there.

"Hey," said Theo, as he poked his head in the room. "Who's this?"

"This is Justin," Jessica responded.

"Hi."

Everything he said was in a disgruntled dull tone. He didn't look happy. He looked annoyed. It was as though he had no way of completely expressing his frustration to anyone. He was reserved. He walked in and sat down in an old lime green cushioned chair. The chair was old and dirty too. He crossed his right leg and sat there and stared at both of us. He looked more than annoyed; he looked angry.

"So, you're going to the doctor tomorrow again?" He asked Jessica. He emphasized the word again. Anyone could feel the frustration in his voice, and the look on his face just intensified everything. Angry and fed up were the vibes I got from him.

"What are you going to the doctor for?" I asked with concern.

"I have chronic pain issues, and my fatigue issues are hard to deal with. I've been through a lot, and my migraines make everything much worse. Did I ever tell you that both of my parents are dead?" she asked.

"I go the doctor all the time. I participate in all my medical issues, and I know a lot about medicine. I just pay attention to everything my doctors tell me," I said very quickly. "Can I meet you there? I would like to see how I could help."

Theo sat there and didn't say a word. Bitterness was the only emotion I got from his expressions. I felt bad for Jessica because he wasn't concerned. I thought he was being an asshole.

"I'll meet you there, and we can go over what your doctor tells you together," I told her.

"You would be willing to do that?" she asked me. "That's sweet. Thank you. My appointment is at 2 p.m. if you can make it."

"I'll be there," I said, as my voice perked up. "I would really like to see how I can help. I get off work at 1. I only work half days because I get so much done in such a short time, but I'll take a cab over when I'm off work. Which hospital is it at?"

"UCSF, on the main campus, 400 Parnassus, on the 8th floor, neurology."

"That's where I see my doctor. He's one of the best I've ever seen. UCSF is a great hospital. Some of the best doctors are there."

"Thank you," she said with a smile as Theo was just sitting there in a bitter silence.

"I'm going to get going because I have to get up at 5 a.m. to get to the 7 a.m. meeting, but I'll call tomorrow at 1, and then I'll meet you there. OK?"

"Thank you."

As I was walking out the door I was pissed at Theo. "He's such a heartless asshole," I muttered. I said it soft enough that neither of them could hear me. I was thinking that she was having some real medical concerns, and he was being so standoffish—as though he didn't care at all.

She walked me to the top of the steps and gave me another kiss. I felt happy, and I was glad that I could be there to help her. As I left, I put on my headphones and started to play the song "She's Always a Woman" by Billy Joel. I had a great feeling. I had someone that I cared about, and I got the chance to be there for her and show her I cared about her too. I had the song on repeat. I listened to it for the rest of the night.

Chapter 8: Our First Doctor's Appointment

I was just getting off work and my phone rang. I recognized Jessica's number.

"Yes, I'm going down to Van Ness right now to hop into a cab. I'll be there as soon as I can. I want to be able to talk to the doctor with you, or at least hear what he has to say," I said.

"OK, I'll be on the eighth floor. My appointment isn't until 2, so you have some time."

"I'll get there as fast as I can."

I hung up the phone as I hailed a cab. It was always easy to get a cab on Van Ness and Post Street. The cab saw me, pulled over, and I hopped in. "UCSF main campus at 400 Parnassus."

"OK."

I didn't talk to him. I just put my headphones on and listened to Guns 'N Roses' "Patients." I was lip syncing, playing the air drums and guitar in the back of the cab all the way there. The driver didn't seem to mind.

A lot of people in AA are against any medications because they are drugs. Some people in recovery think that drugs of any kind are evil—even antidepressants—but they all drink coffee and smoke cigarettes. They're really a bunch of ignorant fools. Most psychiatric medications aren't narcotics, but people have "contempt prior to investigation," just like the Big Book tells us not to.

They also can't see the part in the literature where it says that we are not doctors and we're not to give medical advice—it doesn't stop a lot of them. It also says in the Big Book to seek outside help if it is needed. In my opinion, fear is a big part of their recovery. All I know is that I need my doctors, and I need my medication. If anyone in AA wants outside help, I'll try to help them get it. This is why I wanted to be there for Jessica. I wanted to help her get some of the same medical help that saved my life and got me sober.

I was walking in and saw Jessica sitting on a chair reading *Star* magazine. She looked up and said, "I've just been here waiting. It figures. They're never on time in these places."

"Well they have a lot of people to see. I know I've been coming here for at least the last ten years. I first met my doctor at San Francisco General Hospital, but he only works on this campus now. A lot of the doctors work on both campuses, but he quit working at General several years ago. It's cool now that I have Medicare. When I first started seeing him I didn't have any insurance. That's why I had to go to General." I was speaking very quickly.

"Well, all I have is Medi-Cal. It sucks. They don't want to pay for anything really. Most of the medications that I need they won't cover."

"I know. I have both, but when I only had Medi-Cal, and before there was Medicare part D, they really didn't want to approve too many medications. Now that I have 'Medi-Medi,' they cover almost everything."

"You're lucky," she said with a bit of a grunt. "I'm starting to feel a little headache come on. The only problem is all I have to take is aspirin. I feel I'm addicted to that as well. I've been through a lot, and all of this is just making things worse for me. I don't even have any family. My father died of brain cancer, and my mother died from breast cancer. Now I have all of these medical issues. It never seems fair. Life is unfair." She told me this as though it was the first time I had heard her say it.

"Well, I'll be here to help you. We can get through it together. It seems as though Theo is family for you, isn't he?"

"Theo has a perfect family. It' so messed up that some people have it all."

"I find I get to be grateful for my life today. I'm sure you heard that pain is the touchstone of spiritual progress, haven't you?"

"If that was the case, I would be a saint." As she responded, I could tell she was obviously disgusted with AA slogans.

"I've found it true for me. I've been through a lot too, but I'm doing the best I ever have. So can you." I enunciated the "you" with a bit of a perky lift in my voice. I wanted to give her hope.

They called her name, and she told me to wait here for her. She wanted to talk to them first. She had gotten up and was walking over. I saw the doctor reach out his hand to greet her, and with that her knees buckled. She collapsed backwards and gently rolled to the ground on her left side. She had almost hit her head on a chair. I ran over. She was lying on the ground. She was having a hard time breathing. She was making these little gasps in and out.

"Get a nurse over here right away!" shouted the doctor. "Quick, someone help me remove her jacket so we can get her vitals."

It was like all life had suddenly left her body. They saw the gasping for air, and when they put their arms around her to get her jacket off she was completely limp. As they lifted her up to get her jacket off, her head rolled backwards in the opposite direction. When the nurse saw that, she quickly put her hand behind her head to give it support; then they proceeded to remove the jacket. First, they removed the right sleeve, and then the left. Every time they moved her just a little, her head rolled the opposite direction. She was so small and so delicate. I was worried they were going to harm her with their stiff grip.

"She's been complaining to me about pain, chronic pain. I came with her today to see what was going on. She told me she was having a bit of a headache as we were sitting together waiting for her appointment. Can you tell me what is happening to her?" I asked.

"How do you know her?"

"I'm her boyfriend. I just came from work because I wanted to see what I could do."

They brought the vital statistics machine over. They had gotten her jacket off successfully, then they wrapped the band around her that fills with air and fastened it around her arm. They pressed the button and it inflated with air. I could hear the machine pump all the way up and then it stopped. I saw how it was thumping to her pulse. Then it let out a beep and slowly deflated.

The doctor looked in wonder at the nurse. There was also a medical student who was right next to him. "Hmm, it reads normal," he said in a bit of confusion. "Take her temperature and oxygen levels as well." This was all said with a firm command.

They attached something to her finger to get her oxygen levels. Even though she was gasping, her oxygen was at 97. "One can't get much better than that," said the nurse.

They stuck a thermometer in her ear and it let out another little beep. The nurse brought it up and looked at it. "98.3. Completely normal."

From that moment on, all I heard was a lot of medical mumbo-jumbo. I stood there patiently waiting for any lead they might have. Every idea they came up with was proven wrong by another test. They were stuck in confusion.

This is when I chimed in, "She said she's been having some severe migraines. Could the pain be so debilitating that it renders her unconscious?"

"I don't see what else it could be," said the doctor. "Each test that we run turns out to be normal. Her pupils are responding to light, but too much light can cause photo sensitivity and make the migraines worse. People have described it as razor blades slicing their eyes and the back of their skulls," she said as she turned to me. "It is extremely painful. It is also difficult to see what is causing a migraine. There can be lots of factors, but it can be mysterious as to what brings them on. I'm going to have the nurse take her to the emergency room across the street. We will inject her with medication that will stop the pain. I'm also going to send her home with a prescription that she can use for the pain when it returns."

"I'm going to be with her for the rest of the day. I'll take her back to her house as well. I will help her follow the directions. You can tell me what she needs to do."

"You can follow them to the emergency room and wait for her to come around. Then you can take her home, OK?"

"Yes, OK, I'll do that."

They put her on a gurney and proceeded to take her across the street to the emergency room. Every time I looked at her face, her eyes were only halfway open, and they appeared to be rolling around toward the back of her head. I was really nervous with all of this. I could feel my pulse rising as I was following them.

"What would she do if I lost my cool?" I muttered. I was reassuring myself under my breath that I would get her through this. I couldn't and I wouldn't let her down.

The emergency room was across the street, to the other side of the hospital. It was a bumpy ride all the way across the street. The pavement was so worn down. So, she was bouncing up and down all the way there.

When they got her into the emergency room they injected her with some medication. I sat there in a chair next to her. It was about an hour later when I noticed she started to breathe without any trouble. She had stopped gasping. I was starting to calm down because I could see that she was starting to come around. It was another fifteen minutes until she opened her eyes. When I noticed she was opening her eyes, I ran out of the room to get the nurse.

"She seems as though she is starting to wake up! Can you get in here and try and talk to her?" I asked in a panic.

"You have to give us a second. It is a really busy day."

"What the hell?" I muttered to myself. "It's taking them forever."

I was waiting at the door of her room for them to come in and try and talk to her. I was looking back and forth between Jessica and the hallway where the nurses were. Her eyes had already slowly opened so I said, "Jessica? How you doin'? Hey, Jessica, can you hear me?"

"What's going on?" she responded in a groggy voice. Her eyes were still rolling around a little. She was starting to bring them back into focus. She looked up at me and asked, "Where am I? What's been happening?"

"You were across the street at your doctor's appointment. You collapsed as your appointment was beginning. I saw everything. They were trying for the longest time to see what was going on with you, but they couldn't figure it out. I told them about your migraines. They thought that it couldn't be anything else."

The nurse walked in. She had long blond hair and was very attractive. She had really firm high cheeks and gorgeous crystal blue eyes. She was shockingly attractive for someone in scrubs.

The nurse asked, "How's it going? They said you had a fall in the other building. All your tests looked normal, but Justin here was telling us you have some chronic pain issues. Can you tell me how much pain you are in, on a scale of one to ten?"

"Eleven." She said this as though she was going to lose consciousness again.

"Well I guess you're in a lot of pain," she responded.

"Yes, yes, I can barely keep my eyes open." She said all of this as if a mumble, but we could all still make out what she was saying.

"Well, why don't you try just closing them for a little longer and just rest for a bit. We'll give you another injection to combat the pain. The doctor said once you're doing better he is having us send you home in a cab with a prescription. We're going to keep you here for a couple of more hours to make sure everything works out OK."

Jessica looked up and seemed to snap right out of her haze for just a bit. She was taken with her beauty, so Jessica said to her, "You're very beautiful." She said all of this in a sensual tone.

She sounded like she wanted her. She even perked up a bit and came out of her fog. The nurse didn't know what to say. She seemed a little shocked, so she just replied, "You are too dear. I'll be out at the station." Then the nurse looked at me and said, "If there is any alteration to her state, come and let us know." With that, she walked away briskly.

I sat there with her, doing nothing but holding her hand. I felt a strong bond with her before, but now I knew she needed my help.

She looked at me, and I looked back at her and said, "I love you." I felt nervous to say those words, but I also felt that we were getting a lot closer because of this. "Don't worry, you're not going to go through this alone. I'll be there for you."

"Thank you," she said. "This is feeling much better. Can you come here? Give me a kiss. I can see how you have been there for me today. I appreciate it, and I love you too." I leaned over and kissed her very softly a couple of times.

After a half hour, they gave her another injection for the pain. Then the hospital gave us a voucher to get home, but she told me she wanted to get her prescription filled first. It was late, but there was a Walgreen's that was open 24 hours over on Divisadero and Lombard. The voucher was only good for one ride. They paid for the cab ride to Walgreen's where we could pick up the Vicodin, and then I got us another cab ride to her place.

As I was walking her into her apartment she said, "Thank you for all of this. Do you want to stay the night? I would really like you to be here with me. Don't leave me alone after all of this."

I was so thrilled. I couldn't say no. I felt elated that she wanted me to be here with her. "Of course," I responded.

The night went on and it was complicated by a mind-blowing confusion. First, she went into the kitchen and got some water to take some more of the medication. I couldn't see how much she took, but I could tell she did.

After she took the medication, she turned into the seducer. She was the one that got me to crawl into bed with her. She pulled on my arm and said, "Come here. Take off your clothes." She said all of this with a sincere look in her big brown eyes.

She was completely alert now. She pulled me close and gave me a soft kiss. Then she reached in and really started to kiss me passionately. She was just so adorable, and at that moment I would do anything she wanted -, especially this.

She helped me to take off my clothes very quickly. It was so quick that it didn't seem like she could be in pain. Then she just slid hers off very fast as well.

She was extremely energetic. Her passion was amazing, and I was following along. I did everything she wanted that night, and I loved every bit of it. I was so amazed with how she knew my body so well. She was telling me how to touch her and what exactly to do so she was pleased, and I wanted to please her. It was my duty to please her, and it all felt so wonderful. She made love to me more passionately than anyone had ever done before. It was all so confusing because of the day we just went through.

"No, the pain left a little bit ago." She said this in a reassuring whisper. I could tell she wanted this more than I did, and I really wanted it. All I knew was that this was all so crazy and wonderful. I loved it.

I was in shock with everything that had happened that day, and now I was perplexed. This whole day was exhausting. After the mind-blowing sex, she finally passed right out. I was still up because I hadn't had my medication. I wanted to stay the night, but I knew I needed to get home so I could take my meds, because if I didn't something bad would happen.

Chapter 9: Another Bigot on the Bus

I would always wake up throughout the night just to see what time it was, but after everything that happened that night in the hospital, and along the amazing sex to finish it off, I slept right through the night. I had gotten home kind of late because I had held Jessica for so long after we made love.

"Damn!" I shouted to myself. I slept through the whole night, and here it is 8:15 a.m. "I missed my morning meeting," I muttered to myself. I shook my head back and forth and said, "What the hell." I jumped right out of bed and headed to the shower.

I took a shower, shaved, and changed my clothes in 15 minutes. I put the curl up in my hair and ran down the hill to the number 3 bus. The 3 ran all the time in the morning, and it was a straight shot to work.

I was just listening to U2's "Where the Streets Have No Name" and loving what happened last night, but then I started to have some troubling thoughts. It seemed like she was in real pain, but when we got home, she just snapped right out of all the agony she was going through.

I said to myself, "Maybe migraines are that way." I truly didn't know. My mind was bouncing back and forth between elation and worry.

The number 3 bus came right to the stop at Stockton and Sutter. The doors opened up, and I hopped right on. My music was blasting really loud, but even though it was, I could hear these black kids on the bus. They were headed to school. I've seen this crew before and they were always so loud. This morning I truly wasn't in the mood for their noises.

There was this short and chubby girl with long beaded braids making most of the noise. We are all on the bus and she was just yelling as loud as she could. I was starting to get really irritated. My anger was starting to boil up in me.

"You are always so loud every morning I see you on this bus! This is a public bus! Can you please try to keep it down just a little? It is obnoxious," I said all of this with a rather firm and intense voice. "I can hear you with my music playing full blast!" I really enunciated the word blast.

"I can say anything I want! It's a public bus! I'm going to call my dad and have him beat your ass!"

I took my headphones out of my ears, stood up, pointed my finger directly at the chubby girl and yelled, "Then he'll be headed back to jail, which is where you were born!"

She took a step back and her mouth dropped open. She looked stunned. She looked to her friends and stood there for about ten seconds not knowing what to say. She was glancing around at all of them, and I could tell that she felt a challenge coming directly from me. "You're racist! You're just said that to me because I'm black!"

"Listen, you little shit! I've been taught to judge people by the content of their character, and Dr. King just turned over in his grave and whispered into my ear a second ago, and told me that you are a worthless fuck! I do not judge anyone on the color of their skin! I am not the bigot! If every time you see me, all you see is a white man, and you judge me for it, that means that you are the bigot! I do not judge you for being black! All I was saying is that you were making too much noise! Now shut up!" I said all this staring directly into her eyes and pointing my finger into her face. Neither she nor her friends said a word.

My stop was coming, so I pulled the cord which notified the driver. "Ding, ding" was the sound that the bus gave off when there was a stop request.

"Listen," I said calming down, "I don't hold anything against you for being black, so don't you judge me for being white either."

With that the bus came to a halt on Van Ness and Sutter. The doors opened, and I stepped right off. I was pissed. I was already in some tension from everything because of everything that happened, good and bad, and I truly didn't need anyone's crap. I was almost at work, and I felt relief knowing that it was only 9:00.

Chapter 10: Suicidal Again

I had just gotten back from Peet's Coffee and was sitting at my desk processing all the incoming homeowner payments. The homeowner payments come in at the end of each day, so I do them first thing the next morning. I liked using the keyboard when I entered in all of the payments. It went much faster than clicking with the mouse because I had all of the commands memorized.

I worked at a property management firm that was owned by my ex-fianceé's family, and that was the only reason that I could get the job. I was an amazingly hard worker. In fact, my boss, her mother, told me that I was faster and better at my job than anyone she had ever found. I processed all the incoming payments, paid all the bills, and reconciled the bank statements. I pretty much taught myself how to do this. I didn't have any education, and I did it while I could barely read.

I was also cheap. I was on disability so I could only make about $800.00 a month, and for someone that was doing bookkeeping, that was the best deal that an employer could get. I would get in trouble sometimes because they could tell that I wasn't reading the homeowners' names when I was entering them in. Sometimes the bank put the wrong name on the unit number. The problem at the office was when the names that came from the bank didn't match our records, I was supposed to catch it. I didn't because I would only compare the first couple of letters of the names. Both my bosses would always yell at me, "You need to read it!" The problem was that I couldn't.

I was glancing back and forth from the printout of the homeowner payments to the computer screen when my ex, Brittany, came up to me. She was looking at me as though she was about to cry.

"Can I talk to you?" She asked me this in a hopeless whimper.

I was reluctant because I knew it would be another manipulation. I was so sick of her, and she wouldn't give up on trying to get back together with me. It was something I had to put up with because I worked for her mother. I loved my job. It was a great place to work, and I also really liked her parents. This job gave me the focus I needed to get sober. When I was doing nothing, I couldn't stay sober. All I ever had was my misery to focus on, and I was so bored all the time that I just wanted to drink and use drugs.

I really hated her. I couldn't stand anyone who was dishonest. It was her dishonesty that made me call the wedding off. I can't be with a liar or a thief, and she was both.

"What's going on?" I was reluctant to even go ahead with the conversation, but what else could I do?

"Since we broke up, I'm feeling hopeless. I'm feeling suicidal."

"God no," I muttered to myself. Then I asked myself, "Why is it that each crazy person that I have ever dated tells me that they're suicidal when I break up with them?" It was maddening! I'm not that much of a wonderful person. I can't be!

My eyes were circling, and my pulse was staring to thump. I took a deep breath in and knew that I needed to be there for her. I need to be there for her and let her know that there was no way that we were getting back together. I couldn't! I just couldn't!

"I'm sorry Brittany. I really am. I want you to be OK. I need you to be OK. I still care about you."

As I was saying this in a caring way, I noticed that she was really starting to enjoy the attention. Her face lifted right up, and it was as though she was enjoying that fact that I was falling for her agony. She thought that I was going to get back together with her. I could tell this was an act. Her thoughts of suicide were a load of crap that she was putting on me just to make me sympathize with her, so my demeanor changed in a split second.

"Listen, you just went from weeping to smiling in a split second! I can tell you're just trying to manipulate me — manipulate me like you have always done! You do it to every person that comes across your damn path! Don't pull this crap with me! Suicide is nothing to joke about, and it is not a means to get me to empathize with you! In fact, I have no empathy for heartless menstruating dishonest ho's such as yourself! Don't do this to me! I'm not going to take this, of all things, from anyone! Especially you! Nothing about you is sincere! Absolutely nothing! I can see it again for the hundredth goddamn time! Stop! Get away!"

She quickly ran out of the room. I heard her go into her mother's office. The door slammed and there was hysteria on the other side.

"God, she is so crazy. I can't take it here," I muttered. I didn't want her sister to hear me, and I didn't want her mother to go off on me, defending her again. "I can't take it," I said again, grinding my teeth. "I love this job, but I don't know if I can deal with seeing her every day!" I could feel the energy bubbling in my head.

I heard the door open and my boss came out. "Justin, I need to talk to you. Brittany said that you were rude to her. You can't treat my daughter with disrespect if you are going to work here."

I couldn't believe it. Brittany always runs to her mother every time that something happens, and they wonder why she can't grow up. Brittany lied to her too. She lied to her mother and manipulated her so I would get in trouble.

"Listen," I said calmly. "Your daughter just threatened me with suicide to get me to get back together with her. When I tried to show some caring, I could see she was enjoying my empathy a little too much. I could tell she was putting on an act. That is not something that should ever be taken lightly. No one should ever use suicide as a means of manipulating someone. It is too serious of a subject. What if she was truly feeling that way? Then what am I supposed to do? I could tell she wasn't because she started to have a big smile on her face when I was showing some caring. You can't let her treat me that way. I won't take it, and I can't take it." It started out calm, but at the end, it got really fast and intense.

"Oh, well, um, yes, I don't think that is something that should be used lightly. I'll have a talk with her. It is OK for you to get back to work," she said.

I could tell that I got my point across to her, then she quickly walked away.

"This is no joking matter. Why is it that everyone I've ever dating has been so crazy? I don't know. I just don't know," I muttered.

I put my head down into the sheet of paper and just thought I would try and clear my mind by pouring my heart into my work. This company couldn't survive without me, and I knew it. I do the work of a full-time employee in part time with hardly any pay. No matter what, I will always have a job. I knew in the long run I'd be safe. I wished I never had to see Brittany again, but that wasn't ever going to happen as long as I worked here. I've heard some people tell me that the common factor in each one of their relationships is themselves; but it couldn't be me. This had nothing to do with me. This was all her.

Chapter 11: She Must Really Be in Pain

I had gotten off work and was headed over to Jessica's place. I got there pretty quickly on the bus. When I got to the door and rang the buzzer, it seemed to take a while, so I rang it again. I was getting impatient, but I didn't want to make her angry. After about two minutes, the door slowly opened. "Hey, how is it going?" I asked in a perky voice.

"What? Justin is that you?"

"Well, yes," I said this with a lot of concern.

I didn't know what to think, but my mind went right to the place where she was in pain. It looked like she really was. She was moving slowly and was out of it. She walked over to the gate and opened it. "Can you help me? I'm in a lot of pain. I need to get to the hospital. My head is killing me. I feel like something bad is really happening."

"Let me get a cab! Hold on!"

I dialed the number and told them her address. It was only about five minutes when I saw a cab turn right at the top of the hill. The cab pulled up and we both got in.

"Where to?" The driver asked in a nonchalant voice.

"Can you get us to Saint Francis Hospital? It is right over the hill," I said in a panic.

I was about to give him the address when he cut me off. "Sure, I know where it is."

The cab took off. He could tell she needed to get there with how I was having to hold her up. He sped there as fast as he could.

The ride was $6.95, and I only had a $10 on me, so I just handed him the bill and said, "Thanks."

"Don't you want some change?"

"Sorry, I don't have any time. I need to get her in there."

"Cool with me," he said with a grin.

I opened the cab door and lifted her right out. She was so light that it wasn't difficult at all. The problem was how limp she was. I got her on her feet and we walked into the emergency room all the way up to the counter.

I walked up to the window holding her and said to the intake nurse, "Excuse me, but she's in a lot of pain. Can you help her?"

"Come here," said the nurse, waving us closer to the intake window.

I pulled her up to the window and she stood up right on her own feet. I stepped back a little because she gestured me to with her arms.

"Yes, I'm in a lot pain...." She tried getting the last word out but then she stalled.

She fell right to the side of the counter. She was so close that she almost hit her head on it as she was falling. I reached out and was able to hold onto her. Then I laid her gently on the floor.

"Can you get someone out here?" I shouted.

The intake doors opened up, and a nurse came out with a wheelchair. "Help me get her on here," the nurse said calmly. "So, what is it? What was she complaining about?"

"They don't know. I went with her to the hospital at UCSF. They think it's migraines. She gets really debilitated. When this happens, she ends up collapsing! She keeps on falling! I got her here because she said she was in a lot of pain! Can you help her?"

"We got her. Don't worry. She'll be OK."

"Can I come back there with her?"

"Follow me, but don't get in the way."

"I won't."

I followed the nurse who was pushing Jessica all the way down the hall into one of the rooms. When they got to the last room on the right they wheeled her in, picked her up, and got her on the bed.

As the nurse laid her back, she asked her, "So how much pain are you in? On a scale of one to ten. One being the lowest and ten being the highest, how much pain are you in?"

"Eleven, yes, it's an ele..." She slurred the word eleven when she tried to pronounce it a second time.

"Well, no, dear, that's not possible; but I take it you are in a lot of pain. We will see what we can do." She turned to me and said, "You just wait here. I'm going to get the doctor." The nurse turned and walked out of the room.

I sat there in a chair, which was right next to the bed, holding her hand. "I'm here for you," I said with a gentle compassion.

I was starting to get really panicked now because the doctor was taking so long. "I don't know what they expected you to do, just wait here in pain?" I muttered to myself.

With that, a female doctor walked into the room. "Jessica?" she said to her.

"Yes? Yes? What's that? Is someone trying to talk to me? My head hurts. My head really hurts." She spoke very softly, and anyone could feel the pain in her voice.

"I took her to UCSF. She has been complaining of chronic pain. They don't know what is causing it, but they think it might be migraines. This is the second time I've seen her collapse. It seems really serious."

"Well, let me have a look." The doctor looked at her eyes. "Yes, the pupils are responding just fine." Then he took the blood pressure. "Her blood pressure is normal too. I'm going to give her an injection for the pain, but first I want to get some blood, so we can do some blood tests."

"OK." I said this not knowing what else to say.

It was another couple of minutes before a nurse came in. "I'm going to take your blood, then give you an injection for the pain," she said as we rolled Jessica's sleeves up. "You have very tiny veins. This might hurt a little."

She stuck the needle in and began to withdraw the blood.

"Ahhhhhh!" Jessica shouted. She kept the arm still that they were taking blood out of, but the other arm, her legs, and head were waiving back and forth. "Stop! Stop!" she cried.

It took about 30 seconds; then the nurse pulled the needle out. "OK, now let me give you an injection for the pain."

It scared me to see how she reacted when they were taking out blood, but when the nurse injected the pain medication, Jessica leaned backwards and started to relax. Her eyes started to roll around. I could see it was taking effect. I felt relieved that she was no longer in pain. I sat there by her side for the next hour as we were waiting for the blood work to come in, but I was thankful that she was at peace with the medication that they gave her.

After an hour, the doctor walked back into the room and said, "We can't see anything wrong with the blood work. Everything is normal." He said this like he was trying to solve a puzzle.

"You said she's been having migraines?" The doctor asked me. "I don't see what else it could be. I'm going to give her a prescription for pain. I'll have the pharmacy here at the hospital fill it, and then we can give you a voucher for a cab to get home. I don't know what else to do, but you should have her schedule another appointment with neurology at UCSF. It could be something serious, but I'm not too sure."

"OK, thank you. I'll make sure she gets to her doctor's appointment again."

She was so relaxed. She laid there with her eyes closed and her mouth open. It was as if she was almost sleeping, but I saw her move and respond a couple of times when I was stroking her hand.

Finally, the nurse came in with the prescription and said, "We'll call a cab and have them take her back to her place." I felt better about the voucher.

They got her into the wheelchair and wheeled her out to the turnaround where the all the cars would pick people up. There was a cab right there just waiting for someone. I got her into the cab and told the driver where to take us.

"No problem," he responded.

It only took about ten minutes until we got to her place. I got her inside and proceeded to take her back to her room when she said, "I think it is time to take some more medication."

"Well, you just had the injection a little bit ago. You need more? You seem to be walking OK now."

"It's as needed!" she responded, with a bit of irritation raising her voice.

She walked into the kitchen and got a glass of water. I was trying to look to see how much she took, but she had her back to me. Then she went into her room and proceeded to get undressed. "Yes, why don't you lay down," I said.

She perked right up and said to me, "Come here. I want to thank you. Come lay down with me. Get undressed."

I didn't think much of it, but once I got into bed, she reached for my crotch. I started to get confused again, so I said, "Don't you need to rest?"

"No, I'm better now. I just want to thank you. It's OK. After such a long day, why don't we do something to make ourselves feel better?" With that, she squeezed my crotch and started to kiss me all over very passionately. What happened next was a mind-blowing confusion.

Chapter 12: Nancy

I had taken her to the emergency room several more times. I would always show up for her; the situation and the outcome were always the same. She said she was in pain, so I would take her. I would get her up to the counter, and as she was starting to tell them how she felt, she would collapse and fall. She'd almost hit her head on the counter every time. The nurses would rush her into the back and ask her how much pain she was in on a scale from one to ten. Her response was always "eleven." They would give her an injection, and then send her home with a prescription. We would take a cab back to her place, and she would get extremely sexual.

There was a pattern to this whole situation. It was getting me really confused. She truly seemed to be in pain every time. It looked as though she was. It was so believable that it seemed impossible she wasn't, but she would always snap right out of it when we got back to her place. She would demand sex every goddamn time. This all made me doubt everything she was telling me, but even with all this, I knew I couldn't give up on her.

Because I kept showing up for her, we were getting closer and closer. I was spending the night at her apartment all the time. The sex was amazing. She knew how to make love very well, and she also knew how she liked it. She complained of pain beforehand, but she would just take some of the prescription medication the doctor in the emergency room wrote for her. I was all in because she just kept on getting more and more passionate. She would always spend time holding me. Because of all this, she wanted me to meet her therapist Nancy.

I had gotten off work at 1 p.m. I was going to go over to her place to pick her up; then we were going to head over to Nancy's office. Nancy worked over on 24th and Castro Street. It was right over the hill from the neighborhood where I would always hang out with my friends and go to AA meetings. I even thought that we would go to the Castro Country Club, which was a clean and sober hangout on 18th and Hartford Street.

It wasn't a country club at all; it was just a sober hangout place in the Castro. The Castro Country Club was a hole in the ground, but Dan, one of my previous sponsors, revived the place after it shut down. It was a safe place for a lot of people in recovery. Dan was like a father to me, so after the therapy appointment I would introduce her to him.

I hadn't talked to my dad since April of '92, but Dan filled that role. He was extremely controlling, and acted as though he knew what was best for me. In fact, Dan thought he knew what was best for everyone. That is why he ran the country club. No one else wanted to take that job on. It was always too much of a pain in the ass to deal with people that were fresh in sobriety, but Dan loved to control everything. He didn't mind. In fact, he loved it.

The country club was a necessary place for people in recovery because a lot of them hung out in the Castro. The Castro had a lot of drugs, and a lot of the people that hung out in the Castro in general had drug problems.

At the club, the floors were rotting wood. The walls hadn't been painted in thirty years. In the restroom, the toilet wasn't even secured to the floor. When someone would sit down on the toilet, it would rock back and forth. I don't think that anyone should have ever sat on that damn thing anyway with all the grungy newcomers that were fresh in sobriety. A lot of them didn't even have a place to live. Some were waiting to be accepted into treatment centers. They would hang out there because they had nowhere else that was safe. Most of them didn't have any money. At any other hangout, people had to buy things. It was grungy, but I thought that I would take Jessica there to meet my family of choice.

Everyone in recovery called the fellow members they liked their family of choice because most of us had crazy families. Alcoholism is something that runs in families, and it caused a lot of dysfunction for all of us to grow up in. I've heard lots of people tell me alcoholism is a family disease.

I walked up to the 1 line that was on Van Ness and Sacramento and took it to Jessica's house. It was only about 1:15, so the bus was mostly empty. I was just listening to my music all the way there and didn't interact with anyone. The bus came to a stop right at Sacramento and Polk, and this lady got on. She had her dog in one arm. There was this little girl right behind her. I was sitting right at the front entrance just like always. I really couldn't hear anything because of my headphones, but once she got to the top she tried talking to me.

I thought she asked, "Can I have that seat because of my dog?"

"I don't like dogs. Sit somewhere else. It's an open bus."

Then I could tell she was getting angry at me. She was pointing her finger at me. I took off my headphones and heard her say, "I wasn't talking about my dog! I wanted that seat because of my daughter!"

"Sorry, I couldn't tell the difference," I said as I stated to laugh. She got the hint and took her dog and her daughter toward the back of the bus.

The rest of the ride was fine because I couldn't hear anyone. I pulled the cord and got off right on Jones.

Jessica had given me a key to her apartment about a week ago because I was spending so much time there. She really trusted me. Well, hell, everyone really trusted me because I always told the truth. I unlocked the door and walked up the stairs to her room.

"Yeah, how you doin'?" I asked in a loving perky voice.

"I don't know. I'm just here thinking about the fact that I miss my parents so much. I mean, it is so unfair. My father died of brain cancer, and my mother from breast. It sucks. Other people have families. I don't have any family."

"I know. You've told me before, but you have me. I really don't see my family at all. In fact, I don't like them too much except my grandmother. She is too old to talk on the phone anymore. She seems to be losing it more and more. She is 97 right now. I have longevity in my family. Her mom was 101 when she died, and my grandfather, her husband, was 93 when he died. Some people say that is the only reason that I'm still alive. That, and they say I'm just too ornery to stop fighting anyway," I said that last line with a chuckle.

She didn't find it funny at all. She just stood there moping. "Can we take a cab? I don't feel like rushing for the bus and having to take a transfer."

"Sure. I'll call one right now." I dialed the number. She seemed to like cab rides better, and I just wanted to see what I could do to be there for her.

We took that cab ride all the way to 24th. When we hopped out of the cab, there was this lady that looked to be in her late sixties. She was wrinkled all over. She might have been younger than that, but she was a smoker. She was smoking a cigarette out in front of the building that we were going to.

"Hey Jessica," she said in a very old raspy voice.

"Oh my God," I muttered. That lady sounded as though she was about ready to have half of the throat removed. It sounded as though there was some type of tumor bubbling in there. I had a look of frightened disgust on my face. When things bother me, I had no ability to hide it with my expressions. "Is this Nancy?" I whispered in disgust, turning towards Jessica.

"Yes. She is always out front when I get here, just smoking a cigarette."

I could tell that she smoked more than most people because of the tone of her voice. I was so glad I had given up smoking. I thought it was the vilest habit now that I quit, but I wouldn't say anything to her. I wouldn't say a word, but I have always been told that if I didn't speak something with my lips, my face would reveal the rest.

"This is Justin. This is the guy that I've been telling you about. I wanted you to meet him, and he said he has been really looking forward to this as well." Jessica said this as she was staring to come out of her depressed mood.

I was scared to touch her, but I reached my hand out anyway to greet her. I didn't want to be rude, and Jessica told me great things about her.

"Justin," I said as I shook her hand.

"Yes, she has told me about you. I'm Nancy," she said as though it was her last breath.

"Oh, well," I muttered to myself. At least she is helping her out. "You sound like you're dying," I continued to whisper under my breath. I couldn't hold it in, but I said it soft enough where she couldn't hear me. "You guys go and have your session. I'm going to walk around 24th Street. I'll just look at the shops and find some place to get a cup of tea. You'll be done in an hour?"

"Yes. The session is only 50 minutes, but if you want to come back in an hour, we'll be done," said Jessica.

"Cool. Good to meet you," I said in a raspy tone. I laughed a little, but she didn't catch on.

"You too. Come on, darling; let's go upstairs and start working some more stuff out."

They opened a gate and proceeded to walk up some really steep steps. This was a Victorian house. I watched them go up the stairs, then I turned right onto 24th and started to look for a coffee house to get a cup of tea. As soon as she was done, I would take her to the Country Crap Club to meet my family of choice.

Chapter 13: As Friendly as I Get

The Castro Country Club was down the hill on 18th and Hartford, so all we did was take the 24 bus down the hill, get off at 18th, and walk a block toward Hartford. It was nothing but a dump. I had gotten 86ed out of there so many times when I couldn't stay sober, but now that Dan saw me clean for about two years he told me that it was cool to come back in. I wanted Jessica to meet Dan.

We were walking up to the Club and I saw Dan talking to another friend, Jerry. Dan had peripheral blindness on his left side from a tiny stoke that he had years ago. He was standing with his head facing the right. I walked up slowly just behind his left side.

"RAH!" I shouted and I grabbed his arm and back.

"Goddamn it, Justin!" he screamed as he turned around and put his fist in the air as though he was going to punch me.

"Ahahahah!" I was laughing really hard.

I always did that to him when he had his back to me, and it pissed him off every time. He was always so tense, and he always got startled so easily. His response was always the same. He would give me this fiery look of complete rage each and every time, and right as it was happening, he always knew it was me. He would scream my name before he even got a chance to turn around. He would sit there panting, trying to calm down, with his fist in the air. I would always be looking at him with a grin on my face. This time was no different.

"What's up?" I asked with a big smile on my face. "Dan, I want to introduce you to my new girl. We've been dating for a little bit now. I haven't had a chance to bring her by here yet. This is Jessica."

He started to lighten up. I drove him crazy so many times, but just like a father, he would always be there for me. I loved him a lot.

"Nice to meet you," he said turning to her. "Be careful. This one has changed more than anyone I have ever seen in recovery, but as you can tell he is still pretty sick. He still has a long way to go." Dan said all of this pointing his finger directly at me.

"Hey, I haven't gotten in a fight at a meeting in a long time, and when was the last time I got arrested for talking shit to a cop?" I replied back with a smile on my face.

"Yes, you are the biggest miracle in the room, but that is only because you were such a mess. You still are. Keep on working on the self-improvement," Dan replied.

"Talk about needing improvement, when are you going to clean up this dump?"

"Watch it, Justin." He said this as he pointed his finger directly at me.

The club was a precious place for all of us that were sober in SF; that's why he tried so hard to keep it open.

"Come on, let's go inside," I said to Jessica.

"OK, I'll just follow you," she replied. Jessica was skeptical about everything.

We walked up to the steps. There was this lady I didn't like too much that was smoking on the front steps. Her name was Monica. It was the law that no one could smoke on the steps, but it was San Francisco so no one paid attention to it.

As I was walking by, I said to her, "Could you not smoke here? It's against the law."

With that she got really angry and shouted at me, "People can't stand you! Why do you come around here?"

So, I said to her calmly, "That's OK. The only ones that can't stand you are your family. You're always sharing in meetings about how your son won't talk to you, and with the way your voice sounds because of those cigarettes, all you would need is a flat chest and a smaller ass and everyone would think you're a man." As I said that I started to laugh.

She couldn't think of a response. She just stood there looking really angry. I looked over at Jessica, but she didn't seem to find that funny at all.

We walked up the steep stairs, then proceeded to the coffee bar. The place where they would hold the meetings was in the room that was to the right after the entrance, but we just walked right past that all the way to the back.

Past the bar was a little room which was at an exit toward the back that had a patio. In that room, there were always the same people playing suicide spades. Suicide spades was an advanced form of the card game spades. The same people were there playing that game every day. They were all on disability and had nothing else to do. They loved it. I thought it was a fun game, but I didn't like playing it for eight hours a day, day in and day out. That was all they did. It seemed like a bit of an empty existence, but I guess it made them happy because they really didn't have anything else.

"What's going on, Adrian?" I shouted.

Adrian was an Amazon tranny prostitute who was 70 years old. She was still turning tricks and doing it sober too. She was sober for about 25 years, so no one ever gave her a hard time over it. It was also amazing how she had so many customers at such an old age. My friend Alex called the gay guys that liked people that old wrinkle queens. She was a male-to-female tranny who still had all her equipment.

She was really tall, and today she was wearing a large black hat with a flower in the top. It was one of those hats that people would sit in the sun with on a hot summer day in the south. She couldn't help but trying to look fabulous all the time. She had her leopard print fur jacket on. She always had the best posture. She was also almost six feet and had really broad shoulders. She always held her head erect, as though she was a goddess. I never heard a foul word come out of her mouth because she always wanted to be a proper lady.

Anyone could tell by looking at her that she was once a man. That's what Amazons were supposed to be. It was always obvious that they were because they looked almost like Conan with long hair, a dress, and some makeup. They were muscular with enormous jawbones, and always had such large implants. They scared the crap out of most people. They could beat up anyone, but if you got on their good side, they would take care of you for life. No one would ever screw with them.

The chair was empty at the seat directly across from Adrian, so I said, "Adrian, who are you playing with?"

James, the guy on her left, said, "William," in a deep sonorous voice.

When anyone wanted to know which one they would always say, "William" in a deep voice because William's voice was so deep.

William came up behind me. I turned around and saw him, so I asked, "How's it going?"

"Wonderful." he replied, "I just took an enormous shit!" He had been having lots of digestion problems ever since he quit using speed.

"That must have been wonderful!" I said with great enthusiasm. "It must have been just like Miss Adrian here pulling out really slow. Don't tell me those implants have never been on your back." I laughed.

"Come here and give me a hug," he replied, laughing. "I can tell you always feel so bad about yourself that you need to say such things to people. I wanted to kill you at one time in my life, but now I've just learned to pray for you."

"You don't need to pray for anything. You've gotten all of your dreams to come true with that beauty as your partner today." I said this as I winked at her.

"Watch it, sweetheart. I love you, but sometimes you take things a little too far," Adrian said, as she slid down her glasses to take a better look at me.

"Hey Jussie," said David to me. David would always play cards with them. David was always coming on to me, but he came on to everyone. All he could ever talk about was how big his dick was. He turned off a lot of people because his ego was so huge, but he never bothered me. "Come here. I want to show you something."

"What is it?" I asked.

"Take a look at that. Isn't it majestic?" He pulled out his phone and showed me a picture of his giant dick.

"Goddamn it, David! I've told you not to flash that at me! I'm not your brother!" I said that to him because he would always tell people the story about how he got molested by his older brother. It was something he really enjoyed, from what he told everyone. It was always a disturbing story, but all he ever talked about was sex, so we were all used to it.

"You know I've always wanted you, Jussie. Why don't you come back to my place after we're done here?" David asked.

"I'm good. I got my love right here. Sorry, baby," I said, as I pointed to Jessica.

"Well I'm always going to wait for you." David blew a kiss to me.

I blew one right back.

"These people are a little crazy," Jessica whispered to me with some hesitation.

"Maybe, but I don't fit in anywhere else," I replied to her.

There was one other person at the table, but we didn't talk. Everyone called her Mama Bear, but one day when I was joking I called her Mama Cow because she was so fat. It was several years ago, and she hadn't talked to me since. I figured I would just let her have her resentment. She didn't mean anything to me anyway.

"Well, this is the club. It doesn't look like much. In fact it's not, but it's a safe place for a lot of people."

"If you care about these people so much, then why are you so rude to them? You're not that way with me." She said this to me as though there was a little disgust on her lips.

"They know it's me, and like Dan said, I've changed more than anyone. This is the nicest I've ever been. If anyone thinks I'm an asshole sober, they should see me drunk and they'll change their mind." I said all this with quite a large grin.

"Well it's just a little too grungy for me. Can we get out of here? Will you take me in a cab back to your place? I would really like to spend the night with you."

"Come on, let's go. I can't wait to get you back to my place." I said this with a lot of excitement.

As I was walking out, I saw Steven, a black friend of mine. "What's going on Steven?" I asked. "When are you and Taylor going to make it official and go out on a date?" I asked.

"That's gross! You know, she is like a sister to me!"

"Yes, baby, but I heard you're all about inbreeding." As I said this the whole place started to laugh — everyone except Jessica.

I could tell my comments were starting to get to her, so I thought we should just get back to my place as soon as possible.

"Come on, let's get going." I didn't want her to think I was a complete jerk.

"Yes, let's get going. I really don't like the way that you talk to these people anyway. You told me that they are your family, but you say such horrible things to them. You're never this way with me. Why are you this way with these people?"

"I don't know; it's just how I am. I'm a lot nicer than I've ever been. You can ask anyone here. I'm working on it, sorry," I said as I looked down.

"Well I don't like it. Let's get going." She said of this in a very disturbed voice.

"Have fun, everyone. See you guys later," I said, perking up again.

"You too, sweetheart," said Adrian.

"See, they know it's me. They love me for who I am." I said all of this as though I was pleading with her.

The rest of them waved to me, then Jessica and I walked out of there.

Chapter 14: It Doesn't Seem to Stop

We got out of the Muni station at Stockton and walked up Stockton Street toward my apartment. With that, she grabbed my shoulder and said to me, "My head is starting to hurt! I can feel it pressing on the back of my eyes! It's starting to get overwhelming! Can you take me to the emergency room? I feel as though something bad is going to happen!"

"Damn!" I said to myself. I couldn't believe this was happening again! I didn't know what to think except that this had been starting to happen too much. I had taken her to the hospital too many times, and I was starting to go crazy just watching her go in and out. They could never find anything wrong, but I kept on having to take her. I also didn't know what else to do. I saw a cab driving down Stockton Street. It was a one-way street headed downhill. There were cabs going down that road all the time. It was hard for any cab to stop there. I saw one was empty, so I jumped out in front of it. I ran over and tapped his window of the cab.

"Can we get a ride to the hospital?" I asked.

"Hop in. Do it quick. I'm really not supposed to stop here," the cab driver responded. We got back into the cab, and he asked, "Where to?"

"Can you take us to C.P.M.C. Davies Hospital? She starting to feel some pain again," I said this in a hopeless tone, not knowing what else to say.

"OK."

We were in the back of the cab, so I took her by the arm and had her rest her head on my shoulder. I was starting to feel angry. I had gone through this too many times with her and it was starting to become obvious there was a pattern it all. I started to feel like she was making it up just so she could get some dope from the hospital. I couldn't believe it! I wouldn't believe it! "RAAAH!" I screamed in my head while I grinded my teeth.

"Hey, we're almost there. Just relax. I'll get you in there." I said all of this as I put my hand on her head. My hand was holding her steadily but gently.

Her eyes seemed to be about half opened when she took her head off my shoulder and looked over. "Are we there yet? I can't really see too well."

"We're almost there," said the cab driver. "We'll be pulling up in about 30 seconds."

"Hold on," I said, with a bit of angst in my voice. This inflection was out of resentment, not worry.

I was questioning everything. Did she really feel pain? Did she even want to get sober? What was I going to do if she kept wanting me to go with her to the emergency room? It was obvious she wasn't in pain because every time we got back, all she wanted was sex.

I jumped out of the cab. I looked at the meter and it was only $7.50. I didn't care. I just wanted to get her in there, so I handed him $20 and said, "Can I get $12 back?"

"OK," he responded.

I could tell he was a little pissed because I didn't give him much of a tip, but I really didn't have a lot of cash left. As he drove off, he slammed on the horn in a sign of protest that I didn't tip him enough.

I held my middle finger up to him. I didn't think that Jessica could do anything about it this time because she was immersed in playing her game.

"I got ya, just take it slow and I'll get you there," I said.

I got her up to the desk and the intake lady asked, "What can I help you with?"

"I guess she's in pain?" Not believing what I just said, I asked, "Can you help her?"

I got Jessica up to the window and the intake nurse asked, "Why doesn't she try to describe it to me? So what is it," she asked, looking directly at Jessica.

Jessica said, "Well it's" then she rolled to the side. I grabbed her as she was falling to the floor. Her head barely missed the counter, just like every other time.

"It can't be happening again in the same way! It can't!" the voices in my head were yelling.

I was barely holding her up and the nurses came out quickly with a wheelchair, so I lifted her up into it. The nurse grabbed the back of the wheelchair and took her through the double doors, then wheeled her down the hall to a private room. The hospital wasn't busy. They had a private room to give her.

Then the nurses took her by both of her armpits. "Why don't you see if you can stand up so that we can get you onto this gurney?"

She stood up slowly, and then I said, "I'll get her in there." I picked her up with ease and got her onto the bed.

"So what is the matter?" asked the nurse.

"I'm in pain, a lot of pain. I can't... I can't..." She stopped.

"On a scale of one to ten, one being the lowest and ten being the highest, how much pain are you in?"

I cringed because I had heard them ask her this question before. Her answer was always the same. I didn't want to hear it this time! "Just tell me she is not going to say eleven! Just tell me!" were the thoughts screaming in my mind!

"Eleven... yes, eleven..." She kind of slurred the second time.

I didn't know what to do. We were going through it again. "What the hell," I said under my breath.

The nurse looked over at me, so I said, "Sorry, I'm just worried."

I was worried. I was worried I was going to be going through this for the rest of my life with her. I could tell she was making it all up. I could tell, but I didn't know what else to do except try to help her. She seemed to want help. That's why everyone goes to recovery. They want help, and they at least have some desire to quit. This was nuts because I've never seen anyone who scores all their dope in the emergency room. It would be easier to get it on the street.

"I don't know. I just don't know" was the only thing I could mutter to myself.

"Ok, well, I will get the doctor in here to take a look at you. We will see what he says. Don't worry, you are taken care of." She turned around and walked out of the door.

I sat down in the chair next to her. I felt hopeless. I put my elbows on my knees, then rested my head in my hands. I also knew I wouldn't give up on anyone who was having this hard of a time in recovery. I knew I could get her to see the right way, and when I did, we could be happy. I could get her to be sober. I was really feeling that I loved her. I couldn't give up on her now.

The doctor walked in. He was a white guy who seemed pretty young. It was kind of later in the day. A lot of the new ER doctors were in the later shift, from what I noticed.

"So, what's going on with you today?" he asked in a deep voice, with just a touch of concern. It was weird to see that he wasn't that big, but his voice sure was deep.

"I guess she has some chronic pain issues," I said, not believing what I told him. I don't know why I said it. I just did. I was doubting it all. I was doubting if any of this was real—my whole life in general. I didn't know what to believe because she made it seem too real to everyone, but I had seen it so many times so I knew it wasn't.

"They told me her name is Jessica," he said, turning toward me.

"Yes, that's right," she responded, as though there was a painful confusion in the tone of her voice.

"Well, I'm going to need to see how she does with a couple of tests." He took a little light and opened up her eyelids. "Well, her pupils are responding." He then took her blood pressure and was placing his fingers on different parts of her head. "I don't know? I don't seem to see what it could be except for a migraine."

"She has those," I said in a depressed tone.

"Well I'm going to have the nurse give her an injection of some pain medication. I don't see what else it could be except for a migraine. Those happen without a lot of explanation as to why, and they can be very debilitating."

With that, I was sad, angry, frustrated, and every other uncomfortable feeling that someone could have in this situation, but I knew the control was out of my own grasp. I didn't have control right then, but I was going to find a way to solve this. I was going to help her overcome this. I knew I could.

The nurse came in to give her an injection. She pulled the syringe out of the plastic wrap, took the tip off and drew the medication into the base of it. The nurse had a hard time finding her veins, just like always; but once she had the injection they gave us a voucher to get back to her place. It was safe to mutter my thoughts to myself throughout the ride home. She was high and out of it, just like every other time. The cab driver really didn't care. His eyes were just focused on the road.

He drove down to Jackson Street. I told him where to pull over to let us out. I lifted her out of the cab very easily. I was angry and sad. I didn't know what to do next, but I also had a feeling the rest of the night was going to be very passionate, and it was.

Chapter 15: The Problem with Religion Isn't God

The Dry Dock was a clean and sober hangout, just like the Castro Country Club, but it was in the Marina. It was a shithole just like the Castro Country Club, yet it was another safe place for people to hang out and go to meetings who didn't have any money. Some just wanted to be around other sober people.

There were meetings after meetings in that place. People even stayed there all day just going to meetings. I did that for a little while when I didn't have a job, or had nowhere to go, but now that I had things to do in my life, I couldn't be one of those people.

I was speaking there at a 6 p.m. step study. I had asked Jessica to come and hear me. I wanted her to hear my message because it wasn't the usual AA crap. I wasn't someone who thought that everything was in the Big Book. It says on page 164, "Our Book is meant to be suggestive only. We realize we know only a little. God will constantly disclose more to you and to us." It was these lines which told me I need to have an open mind. I needed to look outside the AA literature as well.

It was all the dogma in AA that got Jessica to hate it. Tonight, I was going to prove to her that my approach was a lot different. I found many people in AA stay sober out of fear, and that is exactly what the Big Book tells us not to do. The Big Book also says we shouldn't have blind faith, but a lot of people in AA can only think one way. They say, "If it is not in the book, then it isn't the program. The program is in the first 164 pages." They also say things like, "You need to follow every suggestion."

My response to that was the Big Book tells you not everything is in the Big Book, and if you need to follow every suggestion, well, then it isn't a fucking suggestion. This tells me that there are a lot of very scared people in AA, just like in any type of religious or spiritual life. They are just as blind to their fear as they were to their drinking. There are lots of people in every different religion or spiritual group throughout the world that get faith and fear confused.

"I think you'll like my share tonight." I said this to Jessica in a very cheerful manner, almost as though I was proclaiming it to more than just her.

"These people are just as crazy as fundamentalists to me," Jessica said.

"Well some of them can be. It's because they are as scared now as when they were drinking. Their fear has taken them away from drinking, but now scares them sober. They can't realize it is fear that is doing it to them. They need to believe things. They want certainty, but there is no such thing as certainty. This is what I am going to share about tonight."

"Well I hope it will be good. Tell you the truth, I would rather watch *Vertigo*," she said as she looked down.

It was so weird: she had seen every Hitchcock movie a million times, but that is all she wanted to do in her free time was watch reruns of movies that she knew all the lines by heart.

"Well I hope you get something out of this," I said.

I had a strong feeling that even though she hated AA, I could make her like it. I knew I could get her to be happy and stop going to the emergency room for drugs.

We got to the meeting a couple of minutes before it started. In the room, there were always a couple of open seats for people. Jessica decided to grab a seat on the back couch.

I went up to the secretary. "What's going on, Steve?" I said this as I sat down.

"Hey, Justin," he responded. "I'm glad you're here. I always like what you have to say, and that is why I asked you to speak tonight. I'm looking forward to it. Like I told you, you are the biggest miracle in the room. I want everyone to see how you've done it. It is important the newcomer hears you. They are the ones that really struggle with getting sober, and you can show them how you did it. You give me hope as well."

"Well, thanks." I said this with a lot of confidence.

The room was very noisy with everyone talking, so Steven spoke up and said, "Good evening. My name is Steven and I am an alcoholic."

People were still talking and didn't get the hint, so I shouted, "Hi, Steven!" as loud as I could. With that everyone started to be quiet.

Steven read the introduction, then called on others to read How It Works and the Twelve Steps. Then Steven welcomed the newcomers. I looked to the back of the room to where Jessica was. She had her eyes closed as though she was trying to concentrate. I felt a little concerned that she wouldn't be listening. I was hoping that she was trying to get in a meditative state of mind so that she could focus. I couldn't do anything from up here anyway, so I just thought I would make the best out of it and share.

This was another step study meeting, and tonight the topic was the Seventh Step: "Humbly asked Him to remove our shortcomings."

With everything being ready for me to share, Steven said, "I now want to introduce tonight's speaker. This is Justin. I have known Justin for a long time. He is someone who I thought would never get sober. In fact, I told him he wouldn't, and that is something I made amends to him for. It has also showed me that I do not know who is and who isn't going to get this program. I have seen Justin grow in all kinds of ways. I am just here to tell you that if Justin can do it, then anyone can do it. Here's Justin."

"My name is Justin, and I am an alcoholic."

"Hi, Justin," the room responded.

"First of all, I just want to say that if you are struggling getting sober, remember, if anyone can do it, then you can do it. Don't take yourself as unique to the point where it isn't possible for you. Tonight, I'm here to talk about the Seventh Step. The Sixth and Seventh go hand in hand. I thought it was impossible to get all of my defects removed, and it is. I'm just supposed to continue to try. I can never give up on the road of progress. God is what kept me from progressing in the program for the longest time. This is because I never thought there was a God that could remove any of my defects.

"When I got here, I hated God. I hated him, and didn't believe in him at the same time, which is a contradiction in and of itself because how do I resent someone that doesn't exist? What I am going to talk about tonight is how the world has a problem that has affected each of us alcoholics. This problem is the greatest of our character defects, and it is the greatest of all humans. This problem is pride, and it is the main problem in religion. Today, I have a faith that tells me that there is a God, and it is God that helps me remove my defects.

"I only have two premises for my life: one, that I exist, and two, I can always be wrong. I would say I exist for both the western idea of Descartes, and the eastern concept of consciousness. I have the idea that both are dependent upon each other. To me the 'thing that thinks,' which is Descartes' explanation of who we are, has a lot to do with consciousness. I have the ability to reason, the power to witness and recall what I experience, as well as think it through. If all I could do was witness, then I wouldn't have any thoughts that proved my perceptions.

"The reason I can always be wrong is much more elaborate: the scientific method, insanity, and the ability to reach for the objective truth, which is impossible to completely grasp.

"Descartes' famous line 'I think; therefore, I am' has been a solidification of existence for many who are able to question themselves. My problem with most people is that they have no ability to question themselves. They are always convinced of what they know. Some people in recovery give me a hard time for questioning things, but I need to question everything.

"It is because of the fact that most people can't question themselves that they take everything that they first perceive to be true. This is something I did for a very long time, and it causes all kinds of problems. It has taken me an amazing amount of effort and awareness not to do it today. I still fall back into taking everything I perceive to be true because nature has pushed me, and all of us, to depend on our senses. I still depend on my senses. I just see now that they should be questioned, and today I have the ability to do that.

"It is taking everything we see as true that causes all of the problems in the world. People do this because of pride; most people don't want to admit when they are wrong. Everyone thinks that they are right in what they do. That is why they do it. This makes it so most people have a hard time questioning themselves. I always think I am right too, so it's not like I'm immune to this flaw either. The Seven Deadly Sins that are talked about in the Big Book—which are: pride, covetousness, lust, anger, gluttony, envy, and sloth—are in all of us. Not just alcoholics, but all humans. It says in the Big Book, which came from the Bible, that pride heads the procession.

"The problem is that in the Big Book it says that God's will is doing the next right thing, but everyone is doing the next right thing. That is why they do it. This is what pride tells us all to do. Everything that happens is God's will because it says in the Big Book, 'nothing, absolutely nothing, happens in God's world by mistake.' So, as I said, it was in the Bible, but all spiritual texts and documents build off each other. They all use each other's ideas, and even if they don't, they all come to the same conclusions. So, I am going to go from the Big Book, to the Bible, to ancient Greece.

"Socrates said, 'No one would knowingly do wrong.' This means with all of the crazy terrible stuff that people take as evil, wrong, or even war crimes, they still think what they are doing is, if not right, justified. Just like I quoted earlier, 'Nothing, absolutely nothing, happens in God's world by mistake.' This means that everything that happens, no matter how bad, it is meant to happen.

"The problem with humans is that we get what is right and what is justified confused. I have done this my whole life, and this is the main problem with the world. I still do this when I lose my temper with people, which I still do a lot," I said, shrugging my shoulders. "It says in the Big Book that pride tells us we need not pass this way. It's our pride that justifies all our actions, and we are all blind to the pride until we have that moment of clarity that it talks about in the Big Book.

"It is also interesting that no one in recovery has a hard time questioning things that they don't agree with, like their childhood religions. This why they are in AA instead of some other type of spiritual program or religion that outlaws drinking and drugs. The problem is that a lot of people in AA are just as closed minded as their childhood religions which they condemned.

"Emerson said it best: 'Each man alone is sincere; at the entrance of a second man, hypocrisy begins.' We are all hypocrites. People in AA think it's OK to question their childhood faith, but not the Big Book. Well, I guess this means I am a hypocrite too because there are still things that I don't question. I still think I'm justified in all my beliefs. I'm also blind to the fact that I am justifying them all the time. I do try to question everything. When I have a moment of clarity, my mind is changed and I see that I'm wrong, but in the moment I always feel I am right. I'm just not honest with the fact that it is not what is right that is controlling me, but my justification dictating my actions. This has only been shown to me through my experience and how many times I have been able to come to this conclusion.

"When it comes to what I know, it is the same as what I pray to. What I pray to has helped me in my life overcome many struggles: addiction, suicide, and insanity. For the longest time, I was alienated from most of society because my crazy mind was too troubled.

"I ran from life hiding in my imagination as a small child. That was the first time, which continued for about twenty years, a life of depression, drugs, and countless suicide attempts. My imagination was my first drug. It was my first means of escaping. I escaped so I could feel good. Drinking and drugs are all about escaping, and if people are addicted to one thing, it is just their emotions. That's all drugs do; they boost pleasure centers in the brain, and all kinds of things do that; so I don't take alcoholics and addicts as any more unique than anyone else. It is with the acknowledgement of a higher power that I began to live in what I now call reality.

"To have that moment of clarity is what I need to get to the objective truth. It is the objective truth that is reality because I believe that all human truth is relative. I need to get past my relative concepts of what I know and strive toward that objective truth which is God.

"Defining our own higher power, like it tells us to do in the Big Book and the Twelve and Twelve, is a relative concept of God, but it is this relative concept that even people of the same denomination have, whether they realize it or not.

"People define God in many different ways. It took me a very long time of going to meetings every day before I found something I could believe in, and I didn't stay sober until I did. I try to have an objective definition of God. I define God as everything I don't know and don't understand; this way I can learn.

"I truly can't comprehend God with the intellect, so I know the objective truth is beyond description; but if I can call God anything, then God to me is the ultimate open mind. I know the absolute truth is out there. The problem is the absolute truth is beyond the capabilities of my human mind. So, I strive for the objective, but the only thing that gives me is a better understanding of the relative. This is because I have a limited human mind.

"The fact that all truth that is grasped with the human mind is relative is shown to me in how all people are shaped to believe that everything they perceive is true. A relative concept of truth goes back to ancient philosophers in both Greece and India. These conclusions that I came to have been out there since the beginning of time. This relative truth is what leads to pride. So, most people, and not just alcoholics, have no ability to question themselves. To not have the ability to question one's self is why 'Pride heads the procession,' like it says in Step Four in the Twelve and Twelve. The Christians call pride the greatest sin, yet it is interesting to me that the biggest problem with Christianity is pride.

"Most of the people that come to AA have a big problem with Christianity. It was most of our childhood religions, and it caused us all a lot of pain growing up. I know it did for me because I was stuck in the middle of Provo fucking Utah!"

Everyone laughed.

"Being locked up in Provo will make anyone hate God.
"Pride says, I am right, and you are wrong. Pride justifies all malevolent behavior. There has been a lot of malevolent behavior within Christianity. I knew a guy who taught anthropology. He told me how the colonialists justified all of their barbaric treatment of native people everywhere they went by saying they needed to convert the 'savages' to the truth, which was Christ. The Spanish conquistadors conquered all of Latin America. They killed the leaders, burned all records of their civilization, took their gods as devils, and they accused the people of being so savage that they were committing human sacrifice. South America isn't Catholic because they saw the light of Christ. They are Catholic because they were conquered, subjugated, and forced to believe it.

"It wasn't these same acts, but a lot of the people in AA felt that Christianity had wronged them as well, and it did, but as it says in Romans 2:1, 'Those who judge, practice the same things.' I point this out because at the time of their destruction of the rest of the world, back in Europe, people were getting burned at the stake for witchcraft and heresy. This was nothing but a human sacrifice, and was nothing but pride. They were practicing what they accused the 'savages' of doing.

"My problem with religion today isn't God. The problem with religion is that people take it as more than just a philosophy and are so certain of what they know. What I believe is that I don't know a damn thing! If there is one thing the progress of humanity has shown us all, it's that we can always be wrong. Thales, the father of western philosophy, thought that the sun was new every day. The sun would rise out of the ocean and be extinguished as it set back in the water. People then thought that the sun revolved around the earth because of Aristotle. It took almost two thousand years for the Copernican revolution to show us that the sun was at the center. The Copernican revolution led to the second most famous equation of all time, force equals mass times acceleration, which was Newton's theory of motion. This got overthrown by Einstein's equation of special relativity.

"It is this scientific method that tells us that we can always be wrong. I would say that science and spirituality go hand in hand. The scientific method is based on replacing theories that no longer work; and all of the religious people don't want to be without the progression of science. Even the faithful don't want to give up the comforts of technology.

"Everyone loves the ease of modern travel. Even the ones that know exactly where they are going when this life is over want the comforts of medicine. They want the ability to get the food of their choice, which is only brought about through the rise of modern technology and the development of massive animal production and fertilizer. The list is endless over what man has achieved that we all depend on. Everyone wants this to progress.

"It is this striving for better knowledge that makes man's progression possible, so I rely on the empiricism that the western world is based on in order to have my comforts, and so do all of the dogmatists if they can acknowledge it or not.

"It would only be pride that drives a fundamentalist from seeing what is truly in front of them. If all it takes to have an insane mind is to believe something that isn't true, then everyone is crazy. We are in the age of information. That means there is too much for anyone to truly explore deductively and come up with a solid answer for what they believe, and this information that we have isn't even the beginning of all the knowledge that there is.

"In recovery, we all recite the quote from Einstein, 'Insanity is doing the same thing over and over and expecting a different result.' If that is the case, then everyone is crazy. The only thing someone has for solving a problem in the current moment is their past experiences. If something worked for them in the past, then they will try it again and again. It is the only thing that they know, and people can only do what they know, or what their experience has taught them. If they don't know what else to do, then they have nothing else to do—no matter how much pain it causes them and others. This is why my definition of insanity is what is the cause of doing that behavior over and over.

"My definition of insanity is someone who can't question their insanity. People need to be able to question everything about themselves. This is the only way to get to any truth. It is the self that needs to be questioned because all human truth is relative, so everything is tainted by the perceiver.

"Some ask, 'Is Descartes' philosophy everything is a projection of the self?' I would disagree with everything being a projection of the self because it is only through the empirical world that the mind is able to develop. My mind, or anyone else's, can only get smarter by interacting with the outside world. This proves there is a dependence on the outside world. I would say that everything is tinted by the self, so there is a tendency to project ourselves out there and have it reflected right back to us.

"The problem with Christianity, and all organized religions, is that their God cannot be questioned. Why would a perfect being have some of the same defects as a human? This is what the dogmatists are stating when they say that you can't question God. I would think that anything which is perfect would be certain enough of itself to handle a question from something that is imperfect—especially when it is shown to me how imperfect I am without God. There are all different concepts of God, and a lot of religions will say that they are right, and the others are wrong, especially Christianity. It is this insistence of what they know that is nothing but pride. How many Christians have been able to witness Christ perform his miracles? It was only those that lived in the day of Christ. They are all so certain of this, and this is pride. Pride is when one doesn't have deductive proof but insists that they are right and only people that agree with them are right.

"There is a lot of truth to the teachings of Christ. In Mathew 25:36-46, it talks about what the individual is judged on. What the individual is judged on doesn't even have anything to do with sin or what they believe in. Jesus says, 'When I am naked, you should clothe me. When I am hungry, you should feed me. When I am in jail, you should visit me.' They respond to him, 'Lord if I knew it was you I would have done this.' That is when Jesus replies, 'To deny another is to deny me.' This is the only thing that a Christian is supposed to be judged on in Mathew. If this is what each Christian would truly live by there would be a lot more tranquility in the world. It's not like I'm that great at it either, but I'm working toward it. Well, hopefully."

They all laughed again.

"We would have all felt better growing up in our households if this was what was practiced. There would have been enough peace that most conflict would disappear, but the pride which Christians have when someone disagrees with them is too overwhelming, and their fear is too great to truly practice this.

"It is this pride that a lot of people in AA had a very hard time with growing up. They felt as though their God only judged them. Judgement is nothing a perfect being needs to do. It is not in the teachings of Jesus that they are led astray, but the fear that they can't acknowledge within their own mind.

"As I was saying, people get faith and fear confused. I don't take faith as believing something I can't deductively prove. I take faith as seeing a purpose in everything. Faith tells me that everything I go through has a reason. If I have an open mind, I can comprehend that reason. People get fear and faith confused because they need to be convinced of what they know when, just like me, they truly don't know much. It wasn't until I could say that I didn't know that I was able to get sober.

"To take Jesus, or any divine essence or being, as the actual figure is when people of faith are led astray. People need to be able to see that the morality of all religions is true. That truth is only something which would be taught as an allegory, not the actual event. Yes, most agree that Jesus was a true man. But to take Jesus as the actual son of God is beside the point. If you are a Christian, the only thing you are supposed to do is 'love your enemy.' This is what it means to be a Christian.

"Every religion has their prophets that have walked this earth. Why are most religions convinced that they are right for no other reason than that was the faith that they were born into? Most don't do the research, and they don't question themselves or God. People need to be able to learn, and questions need to be asked if learning is going to happen.

"God would be the true teacher if the fundamentalist truly wanted to learn. Perfection shouldn't have the dangers of pride that are innate in so many humans. It is necessary to ask questions. Questions need to be asked and sought for such concepts as original sin. The concept of original sin is a logical conclusion to explain the way humans have been so bloody in the past, and some of the bloodiest and the most aggressive have been the Christians.

"Original sin is just saying that there is something corrupt about man given our ability to reason. This is shown to me in what all humans do. It is interesting on how Christians would peach love and tolerance as a wonderful message to the masses for hope, then conquer and kill any that opposed their views and way of life. Heathens, heretics, and savages were what all of those that opposed Christ would be called, and this is still encouraged by the God of Abraham in the modern day. This is why so many in AA have a problem with religion, and this is why it took me so long to find something that I could believe in.

"Christ has one of the best messages of any. There are six hundred thirteen rules in the Old Testament, and most of those were all about what one should not do. Jesus threw most of those commandments out during the Sermon on the Mount when he only gave man two in the New Testament: 'Love thy God, and love they neighbor as thyself.' I haven't seen anyone who can practice this perfectly. They are amazing premises to try and live by. Who could do this perfectly besides God? So, I also shouldn't be that judgmental about them either. This is what I try to practice in recovery today. I also still really suck at it.

"Everyone has fear because everyone wants certainty and security. People need to be certain, and this craving for certainty invokes pride because they are scared. They need to know that there is something after this life because instincts tell us to always try and survive. Instincts tell us that the reason we should live is that life is important. If life is important and we don't want to die, then we better be important. This means fear is the main driver of pride and all of man's difficulties.

"The other issue is that our fear is given for survival. If we are taken care of after this life, then why would we need fear? So yes, everything should be questioned if I am going to escape my insanity. Everything should be questioned if I am going to make progress. That everything is including God today. The only reason I no longer contemplate suicide and do drugs every day is my God. My God wants me to question him because he gave me the desire to learn. Because I have the ability to believe and accept the fact I can always be wrong, I no longer fear death.

"Could I be wrong about God? Well, yes! So I should even question the conclusions that I have made to this day. I haven't gotten that 'overwhelming God consciousness' that it talks about in the Big Book yet. I am still searching for it. I had someone tell me that it is an experience, not a rational conclusion. My best reason for believing in something is that I need faith in order to live in a world that is based on uncertainty. This faith is something that, if we choose to acknowledge it or not, is built into each one of us. Only God would know to put that into us because to believe in God one needs to have faith. This is my reason for believing in God.

"I still have a long way to go, but I'm really enjoying and exploring as I try to get there. Most people believe that faith is believing in something for which there is no proof. I would say that another definition of faith is being at peace with that fact that I don't know. When I don't need to let fear control me, I have a good concept of faith.

"The problem with organized religion isn't God. The problem with organized religion is that people need to feel as though they have certainty and security. Certainty and security are illusions when it comes to our states in this world and its physical features. When I can accept these illusions, I no longer need to live in fear. I can only get to certainty and security when I am at peace with the fact that I don't know. I can be OK with not knowing, and I can see the purpose in all I go through. It is this illusion that invokes the pride and causes all of man's difficulties. So, love an open mind, and love thy neighbor as thyself. Thank you."

There was a round of applause just like always. I felt great that I got a good response, but then I looked to the back of the room to see how Jessica was doing. She was sleeping. Her head was leaning back with her mouth opened. I could almost hear her snoring. My heart sank because I wanted her to see that I wasn't as closed minded as most people, especially some of the ones in AA. I was taking her to the meeting tonight so she could get a solution. I wanted to be part of that solution.

The applause was dying down and Steven said, "Wow, thanks, Justin! I always get a lot out of what you have to say."

Then Steven had someone read the Twelve Traditions and opened up the meeting for sharing. The room was packed, and a lot of people had their hands in the air to share.

People were sharing, but I couldn't pay attention to what anyone was saying. Today I felt terrible because I sat there looking at Jessica sleeping in the back of the room. I was worried, wondering what I could do to get her to see a solution that worked for me and would work for her too. I didn't know; just like my definition of God, I just didn't fucking know.

Chapter 16: The Accident

As I put the key into the lock of her front door, I muttered to myself, "Maybe we can go to another meeting together tonight. I didn't get it right away, so who knows, maybe she still can?"

We had been going to the hospital a lot, and the same thing would happen every goddamn time! This was all so crazy. "Hell, everyone is crazy in one way or another," I muttered.

I walked up the stairs and into her room, then I looked at her. She had this look of terror on her face. "What's wrong?" I asked in a concerned way.

I was skeptical because I thought that she would want to take another trip to the emergency room.

"I can't stop! It won't stop!"

"What do you mean? You can't stop the drugs?" I asked his hoping that this was the turning point that she saw something in herself she wanted to change. I had my hopes so high.

"No! I'm bleeding! I've changed my pad four times! The blood keeps coming!"

I looked into the bathroom and saw blood in the toilet. "Let me call a cab! I'll get you to Saint Francis hospital! Just wait there!"

I called the cab and told her, "I'm going to be out front waiting for the cab. I'll run up here as soon as they are here! Just wait!"

I was waiting outside for the cab, just bitching to myself out loud, "I'm such a prick! I can't believe I made this about her getting sober! This is all too crazy!"

I saw the cab turn onto Jackson street. It started to come down the hill. I stepped out onto the road to wave the cab down. He stopped, and then I told him to wait there as I had to run up and grab Jessica.

I ran up to her room. "Come on. The cab is here! Come on, quick!"

"Look at that!" She pointed to the waste basket. There were all of these bloody pads on top. She put in another pad and we ran out the door.

We ran out of the apartment and into the cab. "Saint Francis hospital! The one on Bush and Hyde, or maybe it's Leavenworth! I don't know, but do you know which one I am talking about?" I asked in a panic.

"Yeah, I know the one. Don't worry I can get you there. It isn't too far," the driver said.

He was driving down the street that people aren't supposed to drive too fast on, but that didn't stop him. I felt a little better knowing that most cabs in San Francisco never really obeyed the speed limit.

We pulled up to the hospital emergency room. I hopped out of the cab every quickly. I ran up to an EMT that was at the entrance of the emergency room. "Hey," I said, almost shouting. "My girlfriend is in that cab and she can't stop bleeding! Can you come and help her?"

"Yes!" he shouted as he ran right over.

The EMT was right at the cab door. Soon another one came over with a gurney. "Come on out and let's get you on here," the EMT said. "So where are you bleeding? I don't see it."

"The blood is coming nonstop out of my vagina!" she screamed.

"OK, well, we're going to see what's going on. We got it from here. Why don't you go wait in the waiting room, and we will call you when the doctor knows what is going on." He said this directly to me.

"I can't come with her?" I wanted to be there for her so I said, "I need to come with her!"

"We're going to need you to wait in the waiting room until we know what is going on."

I was going crazy in the waiting room. Each minute seemed like it was taking an hour because I couldn't stop staring at the clock. It was like I could hear the second hand moving very slowly: Tick.... Tick.... Tick.... I wasn't a patient person anyway, so this was driving me nuts.

It had been about an hour, but it had felt like five. I was worn down, but no way in hell was I tired because in nervous situations my energy builds.

Someone walked out into the waiting room and asked, "Is there a Justin here?"

"Finally," I said to myself. "Yes, I'm right here." I ran over to the nurse that was at the door.

"Would you come with me?"

"What's going on? Is she OK?"

"She'll be fine. The doctor already explained to her what had happened. She can tell you."

My brain felt an instant relief, but then it activated right up again. I was wondering just what I could do to be there for her. I wouldn't ever be able to walk away now. I loved her, and knew in my heart that she could always rely on me. In fact, I was going to prove that to her.

I walked into the room where she was lying down. "They said you are going to be OK," I said very softly.

"I don't feel OK. I feel terrible."

"So, what was it? What happened?"

"I had a miscarriage." She said all of this as she started to cry.

My eyes widened, so I walked over to the bed and gently reached for her hand. I wanted to put my arm around her, but she was laying back on the bed.

"I'm sorry." I thought that was the best thing to say, but then I thought how this is the second girl I had gotten pregnant without meaning to. I rolled my head and muttered, "God, I must have super sperm."

It was weird to think how some men can't even get one woman pregnant. I've done it to two, and one of them is in her forties and on birth control.

She had no response. It didn't seem as though she could. She looked even more depressed than she usually did. "The doctor said I have a tilted uterus, so I am incapable of having a baby."

There was some relief in that statement because I didn't want a child. But what the hell? How could I get someone pregnant who was on birth control and wasn't even fertile? The only other one that could do that was Zeus.

"At least you needed to be in the hospital that time," I muttered to myself.

All of my worries were over pretty quickly, so then my mind took me to a silent prayer that they wouldn't send her home with any type of prescription for pain.

Chapter 17: The Fall

I had been taking Jessica to meetings over and over since she had the miscarriage. It wasn't resonating with her in any way. I was confused and angry. We had also had a couple of more trips to the hospital where she always talked the doctors into drugs. It was so obvious that she was making it all up, but there were different doctors and nurses each time so they couldn't tell.

She wanted the drugs, and then she wanted the sex. Even after the miscarriage, she still wanted the sex. She used the miscarriage as another reason to feel sorry for herself. I could tell that she never wanted a baby. I sure as hell didn't either. I promised myself a long time ago that I would never have children with how crazy my childhood was.

She wanted to go to the hospital all the time, and now she wanted me to go see Nancy with her. I wanted to because I needed to see what I could do to make her life better. That's what it was all about.

I was at her apartment getting ready to leave with her, when she said, "Can we take a cab? I don't feel like taking the bus."

"I would love to, but I spent my last few dollars the other night taking you from the hospital to Walgreens and then back here." I said this with a bit of tension in my voice; like what was she always wanting from me? I had a bit more cash, but I was so sick of always being broke because we were taking cabs. I walk and take the bus. I'm an epileptic. I'm going to be on public transpiration the rest of my life.

So, I muttered to myself, "Get used to it. I have."

"OK." She said this as she shrugged her shoulders. "Well, we had better get going since we're not taking a cab." She said this with almost some type of resentment as though I owed it to her to get her a cab. But what was I going to do?

"Yes, let's get the heck out of here," I said bitterly.

We walked down to Stockton, took the 45 bus to Market and Stockton, hopped on the underground, rode up to Castro Station, then walked up to Castro Street and waited for the number 24 bus. We didn't say much to each other the whole way.

Once we got to the bus stop on Castro I asked, "So, does Nancy know about what happened? About, you know, that tip to the hospital the other night?" I didn't even need to say the word, and I didn't want to. She knew I was talking about the miscarriage.

"Haven't had a chance to talk to her since. I just scheduled an appointment, and told her secretary that it was important. This was the first appointment that she could give me. Everything is so unfair. It has been a couple of weeks, and I still haven't had a chance to see her. My father died of brain cancer when I was so young. My mother died of breast cancer, and I just had a miscarriage! Now the doctor told me I would never be able to have children!"

I knew all that. She had told me a hundred, if not a thousand goddamn times. It got so old that all she could do is mope about how she didn't have any family, and about how unfair everything in her life was. People in recovery told me I've been through a hell of a lot more than most people. My childhood was crazy. I was even locked up as a kid. I have nine different medical disorders with my brain, but I got through it. It is just what it is. Everyone has crap to deal with. Why the hell did she think that she has been through so much more than other people? These were the thoughts racing through my head.

We took the 24 bus up the hill to Nancy's. She rang the bell that was out front. It was OK because we had just gotten there on time. With that, Nancy came walking down the really steep steps of the Victorian house where her office was.

Nancy opened the door and said, "Hi there, you two" in that raspy smoker's tone.

"I had a miscarriage."

"Oh dear! It will be OK. Come in, quick! Let's get you up to my office. Justin, it is nice to see you, and I'm glad you got her here, but we have to get upstairs really quick so she can tell me everything. Go to the Starbucks down the street, get a cup of coffee, and then come back in about an hour."

"OK." I felt sad that I couldn't come in, but I wasn't going to argue with her. "I love you. I'll be back in a bit," I said as they turned into the door and up the steep stairs.

I proceeded to walk down to the Starbucks just like Nancy told me to. I walked in and I saw this girl I really couldn't stand. Her name was Rachel. She always came on to me. She came on to everyone, gay or straight, and she was really fat and ugly. It was obnoxious because people would tell her not to, and she would just continue to do it. She knew I didn't like her, and she looked a little nervous as I walked in.

As I was walking in, William was walking out of the restroom. He walked over and sat down next to Rachel, so I walked over to them and asked William, "What the hell is up with you? How you doin'?"

"Wonderful!" said William. "I just took a massive shit!" he said with a big grin on his face.

That's when I looked at Rachel. She was looking down, ignoring me, just reading a magazine. Then I responded, "I can tell. I see who you are sitting next tooo." I dragged the o in "to" out really slowly.

With that, she looked up. She didn't say anything, but just glanced over at William, then William spoke up quickly and said, "Justin, that wasn't cool. Apologize now! You can't talk to people like that."

I sat there for a while just staring down at her. I was giving an intense glare, then I got in her face and pointed my finger in it and said in a sarcastic way, "I'm sorry!" I used a very confrontational, aggressive manner, so she knew I didn't mean it.

With that, I walked over to the counter, ordered a green iced tea, no water, no sweetener, light ice, and then proceeded to walk out the door. As I was walking out, I turned my back to her and held my middle finger in the air. I pressed play on my headphones and started to jam to my tunes.

There were a lot of small shops with jewelry around 24th, so I thought I would take my last couple of dollars, the cash that I told Jessica I didn't have, and get her something. I was walking from shop to shop, just looking.

I got to one shop and I saw this little silver colored ring. It couldn't have been real because it was only twenty bucks, but it looked cool. It was some type of turquoise stone. The stone probably was some other cheap rock, but it was all I could afford.

After I bought it, I walked out of the shop. Once I got outside, I looked at my watch and saw that it had almost been an hour. I started to walk over to Nancy's office. I was thinking about how crazy this all was. I was muttering to myself, trying to figure out a way I could help her.

I was doing bookkeeping. I knew that I was going to get off disability someday. I was thinking that I would get a degree in accounting; then I could take care of us both. She was in a lot of debt from school, but if I was an accountant, I could easily pay it all off. I knew all of the basics now: journal entries, invoices, accounts payable, and accounts receivable. I did it all. I knew I could get off disability and make a lot of money. I knew it, and I was going to find a way to support both of us.

I was walking up to the building, and then I rang the buzzer. With that, Jessica came running down the stairs. She was running fast. She was in high heeled boots, and one of her feet missed a step. She reached out to grab the railing. Her hand slipped down off the railing. She couldn't grab on. She started to fall faster and faster. She spun around completely in the air and came tumbling all the way down the stairs! Wham!

"Help!" I screamed. "Nancy, get down here! Open the gate!" She had fallen all the way from the top of the steps and slammed her head on the middle gate at the bottom of the stairs. I couldn't get in, so I rang the bell and continued to scream, "Nancy! Nancy!"

I was buzzing the door over and over. I couldn't get to her because of the gate. She had a cut on her head with a little bit of blood coming out and was completely unconscious.

"Nancy!"

Nancy walked out to the top of the steps. "What's this? What's going on?"

"Quick! Get down here and open the gate! She fell and is unconscious! She slammed her head and is completely unconscious!"

Nancy didn't panic; in fact, she seemed quite calm. "Hold on. I'll be right there."

She walked slowly down the stairs as though she might not have cared too much. I could tell she did, but she had a lack of enthusiasm for everything except nicotine.

"Back up," she said to me. "I have to open the gate. Do you have a cell phone?"

"Yes!"

"Call 911."

I called 911 and told them everything. They said they would be sending an ambulance right away. I was kneeling right down next to her. I didn't want to touch her because I didn't want to hurt her any further. There wasn't a lot of blood, but she fell a very long way and had a lump on her head. One of her arms was bent backwards and it looked as though her right thumb was out of joint.

They pulled up and turned off the sirens. The sirens were off, but the lights were still flashing. "What happened?" the paramedic asked.

"Come! She's right over here! She fell down some steep steps and slammed her head on the gate! She's out cold!" I was yelling all of this, but then I saw how I needed to calm down so I wouldn't make it worse.

"OK, I see her." They got out of the ambulance. One of them walked to the back and opened up the rear doors to get the gurney. The other one walked over to her, knelt down, and started to inspect what happened. "Get the scissors. We are going to need to cut off her jacket."

"She loves that jacket!" I shouted. It was her only suede leather jacket. She took it everywhere. She couldn't afford anything, but she had this one nice jacket. I knew she wouldn't like it, but at the moment it didn't matter.

They were very gentle with her. It made me feel better about how careful they were being. One of them was kneeling down next to her; he put his hand on the back of her neck, and rolled her gently over. "She is very light. Only about 90 pounds or so," he said.

The one that was bringing the scissors said, "That makes it a lot easier for us." He said this staring directly at me.

One of them was holding her in his arms and supporting her neck. I looked over and saw how her thumb was bent backwards. It seemed to be completely dislocated from the socket.

"Ouch!" I muttered.

One of them came up with the scissors to cut off the jacket. With that, she awakened right there for just a moment and screamed, "Not my jacket!"

With that she passed right out again. When she had exhaled, she went back to being completely limp. They cut off her jacket and got her on the gurney. As they were loading her on the back of the ambulance I asked, "So which hospital are you taking her to?"

"General," one of them responded.

I was so scared that she wasn't going to be OK. I needed her to be OK. "I love you," I said, as if she could hear me. Then I turned toward Nancy and said, "I have to run! I got to get over there and see if she is going to be OK!"

"Well, let me go upstairs and get my card so you have my number to call and tell me what happens."

"You don't need to go upstairs. Just tell me. Hurry, just tell me. I got to run. Don't worry. I'll remember it. Come on, quick!"

She told me her number. I repeated it a couple of times to keep it in my head. It was perfect timing because the 24 bus was headed down the other direction to 18th and Castro. I would catch the 33 bus which would take me straight there. I was going crazy because I had another reason I needed to be there for her.

Chapter 18: A Real Reason

I took the 24 bus down the hill and then waited for the 33. The 33 bus takes forever, but it was the only bus that goes straight from the Castro to San Francisco General Hospital.

It took about an hour and a half to get to the hospital. I walked into the emergency room entrance, and went up to the counter. "Is there a Jessica here?" I asked the intake nurse.

"Jessica who? The first name alone doesn't help me."

I told her the last name, and then said, "She came in on an ambulance about an hour and a half ago. I saw her fall, so I wanted to come right over to see how she is. Is she going to be all right?"

"Let me see if I can find her for you, wait here." With that, the nurse walked across the room to look in the intake computer. Then she left.

She walked back into the room and up to the window and said, "Yes, we have her in the hallway right as you get through the doors. I'll buzz you in. Just walk straight and you'll see her."

I walked in through the main doors the nurse buzzed open. "Walk down the hall; you'll see her."

I continued down the hallway. I saw her from a distance. The place was busy. General was always busy, and today it was a zoo. General dealt with the worst that the city had to offer. Almost all emergencies came to this hospital. The only time that they were diverted to other hospitals was when they were too full.

I saw her long blond hair from down the hall and walked up to her bed side. She was completely bruised on her left side. Her left eye was red and swollen shut. She had a bandage right above her eye. It looked pretty bad. "Jessica, It's Justin. Are you OK?"

She looked up slowly. It was a good sign that she could recognize me. "I'm in a lot of pain. It really hurts," she said in a groggy voice.

This time I knew she really was in pain. I put my hand on the rail of her bed and asked, "What did they say? Do they think you'll be OK?"

"Look at me. Do I look OK?" she asked in smug anger.

"Sorry."

"Look at my hand." She lifted her arm up and showed me her hand. Her thumb was bent completely the opposite direction of the way that it should. It looked so dislocated that it scared me.

"What? Where are they? Why have they left you like this?"

"They said that they were swamped. They checked me out and said that I'll be OK. They think I have a slight concussion, so they didn't want me to fall asleep. They gave me some morphine, and told me they would be with me in a bit. This is ridiculous! I've been here for I don't know how long! Look at my hand! How could they leave me like this?"

I was standing there next to her. I didn't say anything. She didn't need me to say anything. She wouldn't be able to respond too well anyway, so I stood there patiently.

As we were waiting, a doctor walked up. He told us his name and then said, "I've been told about your hand. Let me see it."

She held up her hand and showed him. "It hurts and looks terrible. Is it going to be OK? Am I going to have any permeant damage?"

"It should be OK once I reset it. Can I do that now, or do you want to wait awhile until we have you on some more painkillers?"

"Just fix it now! It is scaring me to keep looking at it this way!"

"OK, just give me your hand." He inspected it with both of his hands, looking it up and down. "It will heal just fine. Here you go." He said all this very calmly, and then quickly grabbed the wrist with his left hand and the thumb with this right. "Hold on and just try and relax." He didn't hesitate at all. He took a step back, holding her hand with both of his, and before Jessica even knew what happened, he put one leg behind him and put all this muscle into both his hands.

"RAAAHHHHHH!" she was screaming as loud as she could and flailing her other arm and legs all around!

He was moving both his hands backwards and forwards trying to get it back into its socket. I heard a "pop!" Then he let go.

"There; it is back in place now. I'll get the nurse to give you some more morphine. Sorry, I couldn't give you any warning. I didn't want to frighten you even more because then it would have made it more difficult to get back into place."

As he walked away, I was standing there in shock. Jessica was there crying as loud as she could. I just stood there next to her. I didn't want to touch her. But I knew I could help her get through this.

Chapter 19: Who Are You?

I had been taking her back to the hospital over and over since she fell down the stairs. It didn't bother me because I knew she needed it. I had just gotten off work and was taking the 1 bus back to her place. I got to her gate, opened the door, and walked up the stairs. "Hey Jessica," I said.

"Yes, but they were coming down the street. I didn't know the red, but I met someone just the other day that showed me around town."

"What? What do you mean?"

"Who are you? Did you come from Mexico? I was just downtown the other day and we took a left, walking right over the bus."

"What are you saying?"

"I think I met someone who looked just like you. It seemed to be my brother. Though I don't know what direction we were heading—if it was back from Europe, which is just around the corner."

"What the hell do you mean? You don't have a brother."

"I don't think... well, I guess I talked to you the other day, but I was going back and forth from my best friend's place. We walked all the way from New York the..."

I was confused; she wasn't making any sense. It was just nonsense coming out of her mouth. I was starting to get worried. "What the hell could be going on?" I mumbled in confusion.

She started walking down the hallway into her room. "Why don't you follow me back to the pier?" She said this as she stared to slur the last couple of words.

I was walking down the hallway with her back to her room. I was following her with an anticipation in my chest. "This is freaky," I mumbled as I walked into her room.

That's when I saw it. There was an empty bottle of pills on the floor. "Damn!" I shouted.

I took her by the hand and sat her down on the bed. That's when I saw another one. They were both empty. I picked them up to look at them. One was the OxyContin that they gave her in the emergency room. The other was Lorazepam. I didn't know where she got those, but it was her name on the bottle as well. They were both empty.

"You're about 90 fucking pounds and swallowed both bottles of pills!" I screamed.

The Lorazepam was 5 mg tablets. It was a bottle of 60! "300 milligrams!" I screamed!

I looked down at the Oxys. I grabbed the bottle to look at those as well. They were a low dose, only 20 mg, but they were empty as well!

That's when Ted walked into the room. "Yeah, I saw. She's been talking nonsense the whole day. I don't know, whenever she goes through this I just pray something will take her." With that he turned around and started to walk away.

"What the hell is wrong with you?"

"What's wrong with me? The question is what's wrong with her? I've been thinking about writing down everything she is saying, so I can use it in a book. It's kinda creative. It seems like something is misfiring up there."

"We got to get her to the hospital! Help me!"

"I can't. I don't know what to do either. I've been trying to help her ever since we met. It's been twenty years. Every time I try, I just fail. I always wonder why I still live with her, but the rent here is great. I knew you wouldn't be able to do anything either. No one can do anything. With her it is impossible."

"Come with me! I got to get you to the hospital!" I said to her in a panic. "Just stay there! I'm going to dial 911!"

I was dialing the phone and the operator picked it up, "911, what's your emergency?"

"I have my girlfriend here, and she swallowed two bottles of pills to get high! She could die! Can you get someone here to pick her up and get her to a hospital?"

"Is she conscious?"

"Yes, she is, but she is saying all kinds of things that don't make any sense! I've been talking to her! She's walking around, but it is just crazy mumbo jumbo that's coming out of her mouth! Can you get someone here quick?"

"We'll send some medics right over. What's the address?"

I told her the address, then ran outside to be able to wave them down. I was waiting for about five minutes when I heard the sirens from a distance. They were getting louder and louder. I saw it turn the corner with the lights flashing. I was in the middle of the street waving them down. They saw me and started to slow down.

They pulled up, and one got out and asked, "What is the exact emergency?"

"My girlfriend took a whole bunch of pills, Oxys and Lorazepam! She swallowed two whole bottles! Can you come in there and take her to the hospital?

"Is she conscious?"

"Yes, she is, but she isn't making any sense! Come quick!"

"OK," he said.

"Follow me," I said, trying to calm down. I opened the gate and took them up the stairs.

I brought them up the steep stairs and walked them over to her. That's when one of them whispered to me, "What's her name?"

"Jessica."

"Jessica, I'm a paramedic. I have some questions for you. Is that OK?"

"Sure, but I'm going on a trip soon. But first we will all stop by China and pick up some fruit, so we'll have a beef for dinner."

"See, she's not making any sense. She keeps on talking about all these places in the world as if she had just been there," I said.

"First of all, Jessica, what day of the week is it?"

"Monday," she responded.

"And the date and month?"

She told them the exact day and month. She was right about both questions.

"We've been told you swallowed a lot of pills. Do you want to go to the hospital?"

"No, I'm good. My mother is coming over, and we're all going to sit down for dinner after the sunrise," she told him.

He looked at me, then looked at his partner, and that's when his partner said, "We can't do anything. She knows the month and date and response to her name. She is conscious, and she said she didn't want to go. We can't take her."

"What the hell do you mean you can't take her! She swallowed a bottle of Lorazepam and a bottle of Oxys! Two whole bottles!"

"Well, according to the law, we can't take her. Like I said, she knows the day and month, and she said she doesn't want to go. Sorry."

With that they turned around and started walking down the stairs.

"Don't leave! She could die!"

"We can't do anything," they said one last time as they walked out the door.

I felt so scared and helpless. Ted was in his room with his door closed. I felt completely alone because Jessica was awake, but no one was home. There was nothing I could do! Nothing!

It had been another fifteen minutes, and she had just seemed to get crazier and crazier. Nothing she said was making sense, but she still wouldn't stop talking. I was so scared. That's when I just told myself that I was going to call a cab and take her back to Saint Francis.

I grabbed the bottles and put them in my pocket. I dialed the number to the cab company and ordered a cab. I walked her outside. It was a struggle to get her boots on, but I was able to do that and get her outside before the cab came. I wasn't going to let her die! I couldn't!

Chapter 20: Almost Dead

We were in the back of the cab. It didn't take too long to pick us up. She still wouldn't shut up, but now she was just a mumble. She kept on trying to speak, but every time she started to talk, her head would lean back and she would make a little snuffle.

"Are we going to Lond-snuuk?"

The cab driver could tell something was wrong with her—that and he was taking us to Saint Francis. "What's going on? Is she OK?"

"She just having a bad reaction to something her doctor gave her. I was told to watch out for it, and if she had any issues to take her to the emergency room." I said all of this in a calm way.

It was a total lie, but I didn't know what else to say. I also didn't want him thinking he was taking someone that was OD'ing to the hospital. That would just freak him out, and he might even kick us out of the cab.

"Ok, well we're almost there. Just another block." He was calm about the whole thing.

He pulled up to the emergency entrance and let us out. I was practically carrying her. Her feet were dragging as I was pulling her up to the emergency room door, but once we got out of the cab her head was leaning forward. Her blond hair was drooping toward her knees. The entrance had two double doors which had motion sensors that opened automatically. I couldn't worry about where her head was because I had my right arm completely wrapped around her back as I was grabbing her and pulling her forward by her right armpit. My left arm was grabbing the front of her left shoulder. It was starting to get difficult because she became more and more limp, and I was trying not to trip over her feet as they were dragging.

As I got in, I shouted out, "Someone help us! Help her!"

The nurse behind the counter saw that I was carrying her, and she shouted out for some people to come out and help me. As they were approaching, one of the nurses asked, "What's going on? What is wrong with her?"

"She swallowed two whole bottles of pills to get high! One of OxyContin and the other Lorazepam! I have the empty bottles in my pocket!"

"Just set her down in that empty wheelchair that is sitting right next to the counter, and show me the bottles. Can you show me the bottles?"

After I set her down, I pulled out both bottles from my pocket and showed her the two empty bottles.

"Oh, well. Did she take all of them?" she asked with a bit of a gasp. All I could do was nod my head. "We have it from here. Why don't you go wait in the waiting room. I'll get the doctor."

I didn't go to the waiting room. I ran out of the doors that I had just came in from to get some air. My head was boiling, and I was breathing real heavily. "RAAAAH!" I shouted out to the cold lonely air. It was a Monday, and the hospital was dead quiet. No one was in the emergency room turnaround. I was boiling, but my heart felt even colder than the air outside.

It was with this that I said to myself in a faint whisper, "What am I going to do? I just don't know what to do. I've been trying everything, and nothing works," I said this softly as a couple of tears ran down my right cheek.

As I sniffled, they started to flow out of both eyes. "I love you. I do; I just don't know how to make you better," I said a little louder as though there were people there to hear me. I was talking to her like she was lucid and right next to me. "Jessica, why?" I started to cry some more, and with those tears I was thinking about how I haven't cried since the last relationship I was in. It was coming to me that I only cried when I was in a relationship.

I walked over to some stairs that were to the right of the door and sat down on them. I waited there until I could take her home, until they would let her come back with me. I couldn't give up on her. I wouldn't give up on her. That wouldn't be love.

Chapter 21: I Love You

I had been waiting in the emergency room all night. I was exhausted, but I couldn't go anywhere. I knew I wasn't going to make it to work, but I was just going to call my boss and tell her I had to go to the hospital because I was having seizures. I knew I couldn't tell my boss the truth, and I couldn't leave Jessica here in the hospital.

Around 7:00 a.m., a nurse came out and shouted to the waiting room, "Is there a Justin here?"

"Yes! I'm right here!" I ran up to her very quickly and asked, "Is she OK? Is Jessica OK?" I was so nervous, I stuttered the last words.

"She's doing better. We got the charcoal into her system to neutralize the toxins, and now we're just going to be watching her for a while. Would you like to see her? We told her that you brought her in, and she asked us to come get you."

"She's alert?" I asked, perking my head high in the air.

"Follow me," she said as she turned around.

She started walking very briskly, which usually wasn't a problem for me because I always walk faster than anyone else, but now I was exhausted. I was trying to keep my head up as I followed the nurse though the double doors down the hallway of the emergency room.

"She's in the room that's at the end on the right. She's there by herself. You two have time to talk."

"Thank you," I responded.

I walked down the hall into the room the nurse said Jessica was in, and as I peeked my head into the room, she said very quickly to me, "Thank you. They said you saved my life. I love you. I can tell you love me. Thank you, Justin. I mean it. Thank you."

I didn't know what to really say. I wasn't feeling like a hero. In fact, I was pissed. "Why did you do that? I thought you were trying to stay sober. They said you needed those medications because of your fall and the way you broke your thumb and hit your head; but can't you try to stay sober? I know I had no ability to stop for a long time, but you seemed as though you were using those drugs responsibly. What happened?"

"Listen, AA sucks. It's just a whole bunch of people that want to preach and tell me how to live my life. I've tried it. It really sucks. I tried working the steps. I got halfway through my Fourth Step and it made me feel suicidal digging up all of the terrible things in my past. The sponsor I choose was a total nut as well! They all say that they hate the God of their childhoods, but they all seem like fundamentalists to me!" As she said this she went from loving to belligerent.

"I can't do AA," she continued. "I'll stay sober now, but AA is too crazy. I can't take it! I just can't! I don't know how you do! I feel like life is too painful to ever stop using drugs, but I only had those two bottles, and I lost control. Sorry."

"I know how you feel. There's a lot of people in AA that show me what I don't want all the time, but I don't look up to those ones. I can only think of a couple of people that I do look up to. I mean they were all there for me, and pretty much all of them were willing to love me and accept me when no one else would. None of the other people in all of San Francisco could do that with me. People told me I was too much for all of them. That, and I couldn't get sober for about eight years, so I know how hard it is. I know I can't judge you for relapsing."

"Well, a lot of them just judge me if I don't do it their way! They said it's all about an open mind, but none of them have an open mind! They are all too crazy! There was this one girl Jennifer who would always tell me that she loved me unconditionally, and then one day she had some crazy mood swing and decided to hate me! I didn't even do anything! She went from roses and sunshine to a hurricane! What the hell did I do?" She was getting more and more irritated.

"I'm sorry for them. They shouldn't be doing that, and the Big Book tells us not to in the second-to-the-last sentence in the chapter Working with Others: 'So we cooperate never criticize, to be helpful is our only aim.' I just feel like a lot of them are still scared. They're still scared. They can't see that fear is part of their solution, but not everyone in AA is like that. Some of the happiest people I have ever met are in AA. This is the happiest I've ever been too. I can't count how many times I've been in a hospital. I can't count how many times I've been arrested, and I can't count how many times I've tried to kill myself. Now I want to live. I love life. I was hoping to spend it with you. You can do this. You can get sober. Don't worry, I'm not like the rest. I can help you get sober. I know we can be happy together. I'm going to help you get happiness." I said all of this as she looked overwhelmed.

I didn't think that she knew how much I truly cared about her until I made sure that she survived. I wanted to show her that I couldn't, and I wouldn't, be without her.

With that, she said, "Thank you for all of this. I love you for saving my life. Come here."

I came closer and she leaned in and gave her a kiss. I didn't care that it was an emergency room. We were in a private room.

She was lying down, and as we kept on kissing I started to wake up. I could feel myself getting more energy as all of my passion rushed toward her. It was all so crazy, but it felt like love. I knew I could help her get through this. I have always believed that people can get sober without AA. I knew she could as well.

After kissing for a while I stood there staring at her. I went from being tired to wide awake, then I looked down at my watch and said, "I have to call my boss and tell her I'm in the hospital. Don't worry, I won't tell her anything about you. I'll just tell her I had a seizure. I have them all the time, so she can't say anything. She knows about them." I was saying all of this very quickly. I could feel my energy rising.

That's when it dawned on me it's been since yesterday morning that I had my medication. I was going to start getting real manic soon, and I would start to have hallucinations in a little bit if I didn't get them.

"Guess what? I haven't taken my meds in a long time. I can feel myself starting to get really manic." I said all of this very quickly with a little giggle. "I'm going to see how much longer you have to say. I love you! I do!"

I felt the elation rushing through my bones. It was the fact that I was starting to get a goofy mania. I knew she wouldn't like it because no one does except me, so I rushed to talk to the nurse to see when I could take her home. This was all so wonderful! I knew we were going to be really happy together! I was on top of the world! This was all spinning through my mind faster and faster as I felt the mania kicking in!

Chapter 22: Why Can't You?

It was about 11 am, and I was getting goofier and goofier. I knew I was going to start seeing things and having seizures soon if I didn't get my medication. I couldn't leave her there, and I needed to get back to my place so I could take my meds. I spent the last of my money on the cab getting her to the hospital, so we had to take the bus back to my place. We walked right out of Saint Francis emergency room and down the hill until we got to Post Street. The 2 and 3 buses run all the time, and they both went straight down Post and dropped me off a couple of blocks from my place.

"Hurry, let's go!" I said in a chipper voice.

"Well I'm still a little tired, so I might be moving a little slower."

"Well, I haven't had my medications in almost 24 hours," I responded very quickly in an upbeat way. "Yes, but I want to get back to my apartment with you! I love you!"

"OK, I'll move as fast as I can."

When we walked down to Post Street, we could see the number 2 bus coming right down the hill. It was only a couple of blocks away. We were waiting at the bus stop, and I had both arms around her. I kissed the top of her head.

As I was holding her, there was this young white boy with sagging pants that had a radio. He was playing it rather loud. It was starting to annoy me. I was getting more and more irritated. We'd be on the bus soon, so I was OK.

"Why do you think we all want to listen to your music?" I muttered intensely towards him. It was soft enough that only Jessica could hear me.

"Don't worry about it. We'll be on the bus soon. Just calm down," said Jessica.

"OK, whatever." As I said this I was getting angrier and angrier.

The bus rolled up, and I made sure I was the first person on. As everyone else hopped on, I was getting bitter. We were all on the bus and this little wannabe gangster wouldn't turn off his music.

So, I spoke up and said, "Hey, do you mind?" I pointed to the sign and said rather loudly to him as I was looking him directly in the eyes, "Do you see that sign? It says you can't play music on the bus!" I said this in a very fast and belligerent tone.

"I don't give a fuck what the law says! I'm going to play my music wherever I want." He said this with a grin.

"What the hell did you just say to me?" I got extremely intense and angry.

"Justin, stop it. We don't have that far to go. Just calm down. You don't need to pick a fight with him," said Jessica in a soft tone.

She was hoping that that would be enough for me to just walk away, but she didn't know that I never had the ability to walk away from a conflict. She hadn't seen it until now, but I wasn't going to back down.

"I said I don't give a fuck! What are you going to do about it?" He asked with an intense laughter.

"Listen, you wannabe!" I said, walking toward him. "You are nothing but a white inbreed fuck that wants to be black! That is all you fucking are! I said I don't want to hear your music! There is nothing about that that should be difficult for anyone—even someone as stupid as you that wouldn't have a hard time comprehending!"

"Hey bro', what's wrong with you? Chill out, will you? I'm just wanting to listen to my music."

"No! I am not your bro'! I am not a fucking animal! And I would probably have to be lower than one of those to be your bro'!"

"Why do you think you're so great? What do you do for a living?"

"I do accounting! What the fuck do you do?" I was boiling with rage. As I looked at him I looked back at Jessica and she had a look of horror on her face. I could tell she couldn't believe that I would talk to anyone this way.

That's when he responded, "I don't do any of that. I work at Mickey D's." With that he turned his music off.

Then Jessica spoke up and said, "You just saved my life! Why can't you show everyone the love you show me? Why can't you? I've seen you be this way toward people, and I don't like it! You are better than that! You just saved my life! You need to show everyone the same love you show me!"

The bus was now rolling down the hill quite fast. It was a couple of blocks before my stop, but I didn't care. I was loaded with energy. I thought I would pound my ass the rest of the way home.

I pulled the cord for the stop. "I'll see you another time," I said to her very quickly. "I'm going home. Why don't you do the same thing? We'll talk another time."

The bus came rolling to the stop and I hopped off really quickly. "Come back! I told you I loved you! You saved my life! You don't need to treat people this way! I know that's not you! I know it!"

I didn't say anything as the doors were closing. I didn't want her following me, so as soon as I hopped off the bus I took a bit of a detour. I was starting to have auras, so I knew I was going to start having a lot of seizures. I might even lose my consciousness. I had to get home quickly, but I would take a longer route home anyway. It was more of a hill, but I didn't care. I had all the energy I needed. I also knew that she couldn't keep up with me.

The doors of the bus were completely closed, and I looked back and saw her looking through them. It was as though I could read her lips. I knew what she would be saying. "You don't need to be that way! You are better than that!"

I was hiking faster and faster. I always stomped my way around, and when I was manic I flew. The shadows that the trees were casting had started to dance toward me. I could see that all the pigeons were staring at me with their eyes turning red. As they were circling above me, it was as though they were hawks, so I knew I was starting to hallucinate. It felt just like I was high, and I knew that if I didn't get home as fast as I could, and take my medications, I would end up in the hospital again. Probably the psych ward. This was my motivation to move faster and faster. Everything that just happened started to become more and more of a blur as I sped all the way home.

Chapter 23: You Are Better Than That

I slowly opened my eyes. I was still groggy. I wasn't sure what day it was. I grabbed my phone to look at it to see the date. It was right next to me, but the power was completely drained. "Damn," I muttered to myself.

I slowly got up. All of my clothes were still on. I walked over to my charger. It was plugged into the wall. I looked at the clock that was on the desk. The desk was across the room from my bed. It said 10:21 am. "But what day is it?" I muttered.

I was disoriented. That is when I started to think back about the last thing I could remember. I thought of Jessica. I thought about how I had to take her to the hospital because she was about to die. I started to remember how I was getting manic, and how she saw me go off on that guy. I was feeling terrible about it all. The whole thing. Even though she told me she loved me. It was the crazy circumstances swirling through my head that brought me down.

I had to plug the phone in the charger and let it charge for a couple of minutes before it would turn on. Whenever I got too manic and started to hallucinate I would always be in a haze for a while after I came down. Especially because it meant that I hadn't had my medication. When I hadn't had my medication, I sure as hell didn't sleep. When I took my medication after being manic I would pass out. My body and brain always needed to catch up afterwards.

My phone finally turned on. That is when I saw it had been a full day since Jessica and I left the hospital. I saw how there were a couple of messages on the phone. I looked at the numbers that were missed. A couple of them were my boss's number.

Jessica had called too. I dreaded to think about the message that she left, but after the phone had charged for a couple of more minutes I unplugged it to listen. I pressed the button for the voicemail. I quickly deleted the messages from my boss. I didn't need to hear them. I knew what they were.

Then I heard Jessica's voice. "You saved my life. I love you, and I love you for that. This is what tells me you are better than how you treated that guy on the bus. It didn't matter what he did. It doesn't matter what anyone does. You are better than that. You showed me you are better than that by saving my life, and then waiting all night in the hospital to make sure I was OK. I am forever indebted to you. We can be happy together. Give me a call when you get this. I know you are a better person. I've seen it, so don't do that to anyone ever again."

I pressed three to erase the message. Then I decided to call my boss to make some excuses. As the phone was ringing, I knew what she was going to say, so I was going to lie. It wasn't much of a lie because I did go to the hospital. It was for Jessica, but then I had my own medical emergency because of it.

I was starting to panic, so I thought about what I could do. I knew that Chris would be at Macy's, so I thought I would go over there and see if I could meet him for lunch.

I took a shower and got dressed. I then headed down to Macy's to see if Chris could meet for lunch. I wanted to see if he had time to talk so I could tell him everything that happened.

I was walking down the hill, then I started to walk down the stairwell. "Goddamn!" I said in an intense soft whisper, "That is so nasty! Oh, yuck!"

I held my breath as I walked quickly, making sure I didn't step in anything, right to the bottom of the steps. I took a deep breath in as soon as I was in the clear. As I was walking down the sidewalk, I saw the Tea Party protesters again with their signs with Obama with a Hitler mustache. As I was walking by them, a big gust of wind came whirling by and knocked the sign over. I yelled out, "Oooooh!"

As I started to laugh, the protester responded in a sarcastic way, "It's God punishing me for speaking out against Obama, isn't it?" He said this to me in a sarcastic way as if I was stupid.

"Yes, but you believe in that dumb fuck, don't you?" Then I busted out with an, "AHAHAHAH!"

He just glared as me in silence. So, I pointed my finger at him and said, "But all you're supposed to do is turn the other cheek, right? Yet you guys never do!" I started to laugh even harder as I walked away.

It was only another block before I got to the men's building at Macy's. The Peet's Coffee was out in front where I always met Chris at, but first I would go up to the third floor where he worked to let him know I was there. I hoped that when it was his lunch we would meet and talk. I walked down and in the entrance on the Stockton side. As soon as I walked in, I went up the escalator, then I turned and went up the next one all the way to the third floor.

Chris was at the Theory counter with his back turned. "What's up, G?"

"Hey, Justin. How's it going?" he asked in a Zen tone.

"Not too good. Do you have your lunch break coming up soon? I really need to talk. I took Jessica to the hospital the night before last because she was about to OD on drugs, then she saw the bad side of me. After I saved her life, she got upset at me for the way I put someone in his place for being rude to me. He was the one that screwed with me, so I just made sure he paid for it."

"Shhh. Let's not go into so much detail on the sales floor. If my boss hears that, I'll most likely get written up for not keeping it professional, but, yes, my lunch is in about twenty minutes. Why don't you meet me down at Peet's? Then we can get a bread chilli bowl at Boudin's in the food court on the women's side."

"Cool, I'll be out there waiting for you."

"OK, see you in a bit."

I walked down both flights of the escalator and out to the tables that were at the Peet's in front of the building. I put my headphones on and played the air guitar and drums until he got there. I was rocking away to "Snow Blind" from Black Sabbath.

I loved that song. "Icicles within my brain," I shouted out, and then I whispered, "cocaine." Those where the two best lines of the song, so I was just going to rock away, listening to the song on repeat until he got there.

I was into the music so much that my eyes were closed and I was pounding away at the drums. That's when Chris tapped me on shoulder. I took off my headphones and he said, "Hey, come on, let's go get something to eat."

"Cool! I haven't had much yet."

"You broke?"

"Always."

"I can get it this time. You're probably one of the few people that I make more than," he said, laughing.

We walked through the first floor of the women's building at Macy's and down to the cafeteria. "I love these bowls," Chris said. "They're terrible for me, but, hmmm, I love them."

"Everything that I ever enjoyed had been bad for me. That's why I'm an addict, and I'm starting to feel this way about Jessica," I said in a bit of an angry tone.

"So, what happened?"

"Well, I told you she had that fall and she was really hurt."

"Yeah?"

"Well, I got to her apartment she was talking nonsense. That's when I saw two bottles of pills. One Oxys and the Lorazepam. They were empty."

"Well, she's been showing you this from the beginning."

"Yeah, but then I called the ambulance and they wouldn't take her because she knew her name and what day of the week it was. I showed them everything she took, but they still wouldn't take her. She started to get worse, so I got her to the hospital myself. I got her there just in time. They said I saved her life."

"Justin, you need to realize that you have no control over her. You know you're powerless over alcohol, but now you need to realize that you don't have any control over her, or anyone for that matter. She has showed you over and over that she doesn't want to get sober. There's nothing you can do. You need to accept that."

"But I love her, and she said that she's quitting."

"How many times have you taken her to the hospital?"

"I can't even count."

"So, I think she's proved to you that she doesn't want to get sober. From everything you tell me, she has been using you to help her get drugs. Don't you think that's a little crazy? Really, think about it. No one could get you sober, could they? You had to hit your bottom. Aren't you grateful you did? Without hitting your bottom, you'd have never gotten sober. Now, from what you tell me, and what I've seen, your life is the best it's ever been. I think you need to let her hit her bottom. Just realize that you're making it worse by helping to enable her. You've been participating in her insanity. Now it's making you crazy, isn't it? You keep on helping her get drugs. You are trying to control her by thinking you can get her sober. That's all you're doing. You think you know what's best. The whole point is that you don't. You need to admit that." After he said this to me he ordered the bread chilli bowls and we sat down to eat.

"I'm going nuts. Why does this have to happen? That wasn't everything either," I said.

"What else?"

"Well, as we were taking the bus home the next morning, there was this wanabe gangster playing music on the bus. I told him not to, then he told me off, so I humiliated him. Jessica didn't like that. She told me over and over that I was better than that. She was going so crazy about it all that I just got off the bus and ran home on my own. I haven't talked to her since. I'm scared to."

"Well, she was right about one thing, Justin: you are better than that. You know, Justin, I've seen you show up for people when others didn't. I've seen you be there for people that are dying that you didn't even know. As soon as you heard of Jeff, you showed up for him and his whole family. You even spoke at his funeral. You told them that once anyone was in his heart they were in his heart forever. Everyone thanked you for that speech. You are better than that. Remember when Ricardo's roommate killed himself? You didn't know the roommate. You didn't know his mother. You were the first person there at the memorial, and you talked to his mother the whole time. You showed up for people when others wouldn't, and you've made a lot of progress. One of the best lines in the Twelve and Twelve is 'We raise our eyes towards perfection, and are willing to walk in that direction.' We won't ever be perfect, but we need to strive for it. You're a miracle, you know that."

"Everyone tells me tells me I'm a goddamn miracle, but I'm no more of a miracle than anyone else. People told me that and it screwed me up for a long time. I remember people telling me, 'If you can do it anyone can,'" I said in a sarcastic tone. "That was a line of crap. If anyone can do it, then I can do it, and if anyone can do it, then so can Jessica."

"Your right, but she has to want it. She has to reach her own bottom. Hopefully she won't die before she gets there. A lot of people do die, you know that. We're the lucky ones. You need to completely comprehend that you have no power over her. If she wanted to get sober, then you two could have a good relationship, but you've just been making it worse by helping her get these drugs. You need to accept you can't." Chris took another bite of his chilli. "Hmmm. You need to realize that the most loving thing that people can do sometime is not force a solution on another person. You don't know what is best for her. No one does. She has to find that out for herself. When you try and control the uncontrollable is when something bad happens. Trying to control the uncontrollable is where all of the friction comes from in the universe."

"I just want us to be happy. I love her."

"Maybe you should redefine your definition of love. What is your definition of love?"

"That I will be able to help her. That we will be happy. Love is something that I've always wanted. I know it will solve my problems."

"I think you've seen too many romance films," he said, laughing. "Do you know what my definition is?"

"No, what?"

"The way I define love is wanting the best for someone and taking the necessary steps to carry that out. I learned that in the rooms of Al-Anon."

"But that's what I'm trying to do!" I said as though I was about to cry in the middle of the cafeteria.

"I think you truly don't know what is best for her. You're trying to force a solution onto her. To me, all of the conflict in the world comes from trying to control the uncontrollable. It's something that most people try to do, and it leads to nothing but chaos. People expect everyone else to want what they want. This is what every war is over. No one can understand or accept that people have different needs and desires. Recovery isn't for everyone — and how many people tried to tell you what to do and try to get you sober? Did that work?"

"No, but they never stopped trying."

"They never stopped trying because you always came back. You always walked back into a room the next day, you always called your sponsor, and you always participated in meetings. People saw you wanted it, and some were willing to help you because of that. A lot of them had to stop sponsoring you as well because that's what the Big Book tells us to do if someone isn't ready. She doesn't want it. If she's going to be lying to you and keep trying to get you to help her get the drugs, then she obviously doesn't want it." As he said this he took the last bite of his bread bowl. "Hmmmm. OK, well, I have to get back to work. I just want to recommend one more thing, OK?"

"What's that?"

"Try going to an Al-Anon meeting."

"I can't do that! I'm an alcoholic myself! I can't go there. I tried once and all I heard was how the alcoholic was to blame!"

"I don't think you were listening too well. In Al-Anon it isn't about the alcoholic. It is about us, and what we need to change about ourselves so that we can be happy, whether the alcoholic is still drinking or not. That's what it says in the Al-Anon preamble. Try using the definition of love I just gave you. Like I told you, I got that definition from Al-Anon. You should also understand that you shouldn't force someone to do something they don't want or aren't ready for. Don't worry; you can do what you want. I'm just giving you a suggestion that worked for me. I got to run back to work. I love you, and you can call me later if you like." As Chris said this, he got up and left very quickly.

I didn't know what to do, but I wasn't going to go to an Al-Anon meeting. I couldn't! I just couldn't! "I'm going to stay with Jessica," I muttered to myself. "I can't leave her. I love her. I do want the best for her. I can't walk away from someone I love. I can't."

I sat at the table just picking at my bowl. I hadn't eaten anything in one-and-a-half days, but because of all of this I wasn't too hungry. That's when my phone rang. My heart jumped into my chest. I was in the midst of a nervous anticipation as I pulled it out of my pocket. I was thinking it was going to be her, but I didn't know if I wanted to talk yet. I didn't want to face her. I didn't think that I could. I was so scared of what she was thinking of me, but I also had to talk to her.

I looked at the phone and saw it was her. I knew I had to answer because I wanted to continue to be with her. "Hello," I said in a soft shy whisper.

"Hey, where are you? I called a couple of times. I even left a message. Can I talk to you? I just want to talk," said Jessica.

"Well, I'm at Macy's right now. I just woke up a couple of hours ago. Once I got home, I took my meds and passed out for a day."

"Well, can I talk to you? Can I see you?"

"Why don't you come over to my apartment? I'll be back there in about 15 minutes."

"OK, but it will take me about an hour to get there. Can you head back? Then I'll ring your bell, and you can buzz me in."

"Sure."

"I'll see you in an hour. I love you, and you saved my life, but I want to talk to you."

I was scared. I couldn't tell her I loved her back because I was so scared, so I just responded, "OK, see you in a bit."

As I hung up the phone, a sense of dread came over me. I was so scared of what she was going to say to me. What could I say back?

Chapter 24: Why

I sat waiting in a nervous tension in my apartment. I was so scared of what she was going to say to me, and I didn't know exactly what I was going to tell her. I wanted her to love me, and I knew that she couldn't be around any of my vicious behavior.

Ever since I was a kid, and all that I went through, I had this amazing capacity to humble anyone. I was sober for a couple of years now, but alcohol and drugs were no longer my issue. Chris had told me many times that I was more addicted to putting people in their place then I ever was to drugs or alcohol. I got such a high out of feeling superior to people. I only knew this because people told me they could see it. I trusted what they said because the people in recovery knew more about me than I did about myself.

It was true: I got this amazing sense of power and domination out of conquering other people. I would always have the last laugh. It was the only way that I could truly feel safe. I always felt that I needed to protect myself. I made a vow to myself as a child that no one would ever hurt me again; if they did, they would pay for it. Chris had pointed out to me over and over that I always wanted to be a part of. I wanted acceptance. He always told me I was so scared of people.

Mulling all of this over, the buzzer to the building entrance rang.

I picked up the phone and asked, "Hey, is that you?"

"Yes, it's Jessica. Can you buzz me in so we can talk?" With that, I just hit number 9 and buzzed the door open.

It was only about minute until I heard a knock at the door. I was on the fifth floor, the first apartment to the left of the elevator. It was an old elevator with a metal door that you had to open and close yourself. It was slow, but my apartment was right next to it so it didn't take her long.

I opened it and said, "Hey." I said this looking down.

I couldn't even look her in the eyes. I was scared of what she was going to say to me.

"Can you come in?" I told her.

With that I backed up and let her walk softly into the apartment. I didn't know what she was thinking, but I was trying to figure it out with every movement of her body and every expression on her face. She was staring at me. I kept on looking away because I was so nervous. She didn't seem angry, just upset.

"Sorry," I said, looking down. "I don't know, it's just, well, it's just, he screwed with me first." I wanted to explain to her why I was this way.

"You saved my life," she said, looking softly into my eyes.

When she said this, I felt a little relaxation come through me, but then I tensed right up again. I felt as though there would be this "but" after that, and she would say that she couldn't be with anyone as vicious as me.

"You saved my life, but I want to know why do you talk to people like that? If you are willing to save my life, and show me unconditional love, then can't you show everyone that side of you? You've done all kinds of things for me. You are an amazing person, so what is this stuff about?"

"I don't know. I've just made sure that no one ever gets the best of me. He started it, so I put him in his place."

"But I've seen you be this way even with some of the people that you call your friends. Why do you do that?"

"I can't really explain it. I've never been able not to say something that I'm thinking. That's the reason that I'm always muttering to myself. Let me tell you, I've had doctors and psychiatrists ask me how I think of the insults that I think of. Richard, my current psychiatrist, said that my verbal IQ with insults is about 160. That's a genius level. He told me he's never seen anyone who can think of the things I do. I think of them in a split second as well. I can't control myself, and when someone is rude to me I just fire back. I've never met anyone I couldn't conquer with my words. I mean, I got beat up a lot because of it, but they always walk away angry, so it was like I always won."

"That's not winning. That's just hurtful. You don't do it to me, so why do you do it to other people?"

"I can't explain that either. There are just some people that I have never given a hard time to. I can't explain any of it. Can I show you something? It's something I wrote when I was a kid. I wrote a whole book actually."

"I thought you could barely read; how were you able to write a book?"

"It's just poetry. I had other people do the spell check. Take a look at some of them, will you?"

"OK," she said this quite softly.

I walked over to my desk and pulled out a leather notebook. All of my poems were printed out and kept immaculate. The paper was printed out 15 years ago, and the disks that they were saved on were no longer any good, but the hard copies were without a wrinkle.

"Here, take a look at this one," I said.

I handed it to her. This poem was called "Why." I felt as though it would explain a little. She began to read it out loud:

> my remorsed conscience shamed,
> in soothing songs which they lack,
> from bitter feelings lamed
> to a loveless, grim heart of black.
>
> by vision sweetened myth,
> since before one spoke to me,
> in twilight blissful with
> her arms willing, open and free.
>
> in hopeless dirgeful tears,
> i acquit all i attack,
> just upon sullen fears
> of emotions, which i do lack.

She looked up and said, "That's amazing. It is extremely dark, and it is almost sociopathic. I'm a writer, and I've never been able to write in iambic pentameter. That's really hard. How did you do that without being able to read? It's dated April 3, 1993. How old were you?"

"Fifteen. I don't know how I was able to write that way. It just came out." I stared to perk up a little bit because I saw how enthusiastic that she got.

"Well it just seemed as though your heart was broken as a child. You talk about how you love someone in here. How she's willing to accept you, but then you are pulled away because of the way you fight. I feel like that is happening with us. It's amazing. It tells how you lash out at people. I mean I can understand that, but you are such a good person. You truly don't need to treat people this way. I feel like I can understand you a bit better now. Can I ask you why there are no capital letters?"

"It had to do with my self-worth. I was really depressed as a child. I was suicidal. Hell, I was suicidal for most of my life. That's why I got sent to that school. It was there that I made sure that no one ever hurt me again. I wasn't big, but I was the bully. If anyone tried to beat me up they would just get in trouble. I learned how to protect myself at that school. No one would mess with me. I was one of the smallest there, but I was the toughest. I learned there not to let anyone get the best of me. If you can tell, that's what this poem is about."

"I see that, and I understand it, but that can't be you anymore. I don't think that it ever was. You were just hurt, but now it is time to let that go. I love you, and I want you to know that. Come here, let's lay down on your bed." She gently grabbed me by the hand and pulled me onto the bed. "I want you to promise me something. Can you, please?"

I was excited and nervous all at the same time. I didn't want her to have me promise something that I couldn't keep, but I said, "OK. I mean, well, OK."

As she pulled me onto the bed, she gave me a kiss. "Lie down with me. I want you to promise me something." She gave me another kiss and then said, "Try and treat everyone with the same love you treat me. I know you can. I can see it in you. You can do this."

I could feel that there was still a connection, but I made sure I didn't respond to her because I didn't want to promise anything I couldn't keep. The only thing she did for the rest of the day was hold me in bed.

Chapter 25: Things Are Good

I woke up in the bed with Jessica in my arms. We had been holding each other all night. I was feeling wonderful about the way we made up; how I showed her that poem because I felt that she understood me better now. I sensed that this took our relationship to another level. I could feel that we were finally getting to the point where she wouldn't want any more drugs. She had told me she didn't because she came so close to dying. I loved her, and I knew we would get through all of this and be happy together. I was at peace with these thoughts. They calmed the anxiety in my mind. No matter what happened, I knew that we would make it together.

"I love you," I muttered, as I lifted my head just a little bit to get a better look at her. "Hey, Jessica, wake up. Hey, I have to get to work. Can we meet later today? I'm off at 2. All I need to do is catch up on all the stuff in the office. I told my boss I would put in a little more time, and then we can meet. Is that cool? I always get things done quickly, so it won't take me too long at all."

"What? Oh, yeah, that's cool. I'm going to go home in just a little bit so I can take a shower and get cleaned up. Would you be willing to take me to see Nancy when you're off of work? The appointment is at 4:30. She told me in a message yesterday that she wanted to see you again as well. Is that OK?"

"Of course," I said, perking right up. "Here, let me give you a key. You can come in and go as you like just like I do at your place. I love you, and I want you to know that."

"Thanks. I love you too."

With that, I ran into the shower and got ready in about fifteen minutes.

"Just meet me back here, will you? I'll be back at about 2:30. Then we can go to Starbucks down the street. We'll just walk to the underground and make our way back up to the Castro. Is that cool?"

"Sure," she said, as I woke up a little bit more.

I saw a twinkle in her eye. I was happy. Despite the hospital and the bus on the way back, we were getting along great. Everything was working out. This felt so great as I ran out the door, down the hill to Sutter, and hopped on the number 3 bus. I was thinking about how all this was working out on my way to work as I was listening to "One" by U2.

Chapter 26: On Purpose?

I had picked up Jessica at my apartment; we walked down to Powell Street Station, and took the K underground to the Castro. We walked upstairs to the street and hopped on the 24 bus and rode it up the hill to 24th. We weren't talking much. I just had my arm around her, and I was feeling really good. After I saved her life, I knew she hit the bottom that she needed to. I felt as though now she would start to stay sober.

We got off the bus and walked to the office building. She rang the buzzer to let Nancy know we were there. I looked at the steps. The steep steps that she had fallen down. I was nervous that she might not want to go up them, but it didn't seem like a problem to her. I don't think she cared, but it was still worrying me.

Nancy buzzed the door open and we walked up. We got to the top of the steps. It was cool that we were right on time. After we walked into the waiting room she rang the bell to her office, and we just sat on the couch waiting for Nancy.

I knew that I was going to help her get through everything. That's when I turned to her and said, "You know, I am really going to be trying hard to treat everyone with the love I treat you."

"That's wonderful. Come here and give me a kiss."

I leaned over and kissed her very passionately.

It was interesting because Nancy was about five minutes late. She never did this before, but then the door started to creak slowly open. Nancy stepped out of her office door. "Come on in, both of you. I need to tell you both something. I want Justin to hear this too," she said in her raspy voice.

She didn't look very happy. She seemed very standoffish, as though there was something serious going on. "Well, Jessica," she said. "I have a report from General Hospital, and it told me something. I'm sorry to tell you, and Justin, you need to listen too, I can't work with you anymore."

"What?" Shouted out Jessica. "Why not? What did I do?"

"You know what you did. You threw yourself down the stairs. You threw yourself down these steep stairs so you could get drugs. You have gone to every emergency room in this town using this injury to get you more painkillers and benzos. You are put on a federal list now, and if you show up to an emergency room in pain asking for drugs, they will refuse you. All they have to do is enter in your name and a warning will pop up."

Then Nancy turned to me and said, "Justin, you have been trying to help her, but what she needs right now is for you to detach from her and let her have her own consequences. You need to break up with her and not enable her anymore. You have been by her side taking her to these emergency rooms, and the only thing that is doing is making her live even deeper in her disease. Justin, you should try an Al-Anon meeting. I know it is hard to hear, but you have to accept this as well."

I didn't know what to do. I was shocked. That's when I replied in a confronting tone, "She couldn't have thrown herself down the stairs; she's a hypochondriac! She didn't need to! Whenever she wanted something, I saw her talk doctors into it!" I couldn't believe what I was hearing, and I felt I had to stick up for Jessica.

Then Nancy replied, "Well, even if she didn't, she is still abusing the drugs that she is getting from the emergency room. That, and you have been the one helping her get it. This is something that I have seen before, Justin. Some people score all their dope in the emergency room. Jessica can't be honest with anyone, including herself; and you need to get honest with yourself as well. You can't save her. Only she can do this work, and that is why I can't work with her anymore either. She's been lying to me the whole time too. I can't work with a patient if they lie to me. If she really doesn't want to use drugs anymore, she is going to have the desire to stop. She is going to need to be completely honest with herself and everyone else. Most addicts can't tell the truth, and Jessica here is very good at lying. I fell for a lot of it too, but I have had a chance to talk to her doctors, and we all agree that she needs to find her way out of this. If she wants help, she can get it, but the desire has to come from her. She can't be lying to people anymore to get what she wants. She was lying to me this whole time, and what did I do? I would just try to help her get better, but she only wanted me to enable her. I can't do that. That would be against my profession."

"This is unethical!" Jessica screamed. "You are my therapist! And you aren't supposed to divulge anything to anyone! I could sue you!"

"I don't know how; you can't even afford a lawyer. That, and you have brought Justin into our sessions before. I thought it would only be fair to him with what you are doing to him, to me, and to yourself. Justin needs to know because he's part of the problem too. It is up to him what he does next, but I know I can't contribute anymore," replied Nancy.

I was there in shock. I thought that she was telling me the truth for the first time about her pain. Then I thought that she really did need it this time, but I couldn't believe how many times she went to the emergency room. She had gone to the emergency room without me as well. I had gotten really angry, but I didn't know who to be angry at. I wanted to be angry at Jessica, but I couldn't. I didn't think it was right for Nancy to divulge what was supposed to be between her and a client, but I also wanted to know.

"Screw you!" Jessica shouted, "You shouldn't tell anyone my medical business!"

"Well, we've talked enough. I need to get going. Why don't you leave now. And Justin?"

"Yes?" I said in a tense angry and confused tone.

"You're contributing. You need to go your own way so she can discover what she needs to on her own. Life is about learning, and you're keeping her from what she needs to learn." With that she turned around, walked back into her office, and closed the door.

"Come on, let's go." I said this not knowing what to say. I said this knowing that I couldn't give up on her. "You're right, she shouldn't have told me," I said in a weepy tone.

"She shouldn't have! I can't believe this! Doesn't she know how much I've been through! My parents are both dead! I hardly have any money! I was paying her, and now she goes out and violates my contract with her! She shouldn't have done this! Tell me she shouldn't have done this!"

I couldn't resist. I didn't know what to say except to agree with her. "Yeah, I guess she shouldn't have."

I was angry. I was angry at Jessica. I was angry at myself for falling for all of this. Even though I was angry, I still couldn't walk away from her. I couldn't do what Nancy said I should. I couldn't detach. I didn't even know what she meant by detaching. I knew that if I loved someone I would be there for them no matter what. I would always be there for her because I wanted her to get better. I was going to help her get through this part of her life. I had a feeling we would be happy together some day. I knew it. I knew it, but I was still confused. I didn't know how to help her, and I wasn't going to give up.

"What am I supposed to do now?" I muttered under my breath.

"What did you say? What was that?" She shouted at me.

"Nothing. I didn't say anything."

Chapter 27: The Hospital Again?

Despite all that happened with Nancy, and her telling me about the abuse of the emergency room, I felt relieved that she could no longer get drugs. I knew she had been making it up every time that she went to the hospital, except when she fell. I didn't think that she threw herself down the stairs. She was always worried about injuring herself, and she was the best actress that I had ever met. She didn't need to injure herself. I saw her talk doctors into drugs so many times that I knew she could get them whenever she wanted. I did believe that once she fell, she was using it as an excuse to get more, but no way in hell could she do that on purpose.

I had gotten off work at noon. I was headed over to Jessica's. I really wanted to see her and see what I could do to get her out of her funk now that she no longer had a therapist. I walked up to Sacramento Street and took the 1 bus.

Once I got to her place, I unlocked the door and walked right in. I walked up the stairs to her bedroom. "Hey, how are you? What's going on?" I asked her.

"Huh? What's that? Is that you, Justin?"

"Yes," I said slowly. "What's up?" I felt nervous because she was lying on the bed as though she had a hard time seeing. I was hoping she wasn't going to tell me she had a migraine.

I took a deep breath and then asked, "You OK?" I was really anxious.

"I'm having a hard time seeing." She slurred the "ing."

I had seen this a million times now! I didn't know what to do! I was just hoping she wouldn't ask me to take her to the hospital! I was starting to get really mad. Then it just switched to depression. I was helpless.

"Is there something I can do?" I asked this even though I knew her response. I knew what she was going to say. I was almost angry, but then I just got really sad. I couldn't be angry at her.

She responded, "Would you please take me to the hospital? I'm having a hard time seeing. I can't even walk that far without falling. I barely made it to the bathroom earlier. I'm in a lot of pain. Can you please?"

"Can you make it on the bus?" I asked this because I didn't have a lot of money left. I didn't get paid for another week, and I needed every bit of my cash to last.

"I don't think I can make it. Can we please take a cab? I just can't make it on the bus."

"OK," I said as I choked. "Let me call one. Just wait there for a second, then I'll carry you down the stairs."

"Thank you, I love you, and thank you very much."

"Yeah, OK, whatever."

I called the cab. They said they would be out in front in fifteen minutes. I lifted her out of bed. I could carry her anywhere, and I had done that a million times. Caring her was never the problem. I felt just as helpless as she was acting. I lifted her up and put her clothes on. She was acting just like a limp piece of string, but it was always so easy to get her dressed.

I carried her right down the stairs. The cab wouldn't be there for another five minutes, but I could just rest her petite frame on the cement steps. It was insanity.

The cab ride was quick. Once it pulled up, I lifted her out of the cab to get into the emergency room entrance. As I was carrying her, she said to me. "I think I'm getting a little stronger. I can walk a little better now."

She was still holding onto me as we got to the counter. It wasn't busy at all. It was the middle of the day on a weekday. I knew what was going to happen next.

She got up to the counter and then said, "Yes, I can barely see right now; can you help me. I'm in a lot of pain. I have a, a, mirgra…"

With that, I foresaw everything that was going to happen. I foresaw what she was going to do. As she was slurring the word migraine, she fell to the side. She barely missed her head on the counter. I reached out and grabbed her, like I had done so many times now, and just eased her down on the floor.

The nurses came running out. They all seemed so concerned. They were concerned, but I knew she was fine. Nothing was wrong, nothing except her addiction. That was the only problem. I felt a little better that, even though I knew she was lying, she was on that list. She was on that federal list, so I felt safe in one way or another.

"Come quick! Lift her up into this wheelchair!" The nurse said to me. I lifted her right off the floor onto the wheelchair. It was extremely easy, but very difficult at the same time.

Then nurse leaned over to her and asked, "How much pain are you in, on a scale from one to ten?"

I knew the answer. I always knew the answer, but I also knew that she was in that computer system, so I was hoping she would snap out of it once they told her no!

"Eleven! Elev..." She shouted the first time, but then dribbled the second one into another slur.

"I'll get the doctor. Just wait here sweetie," the nurse said this in a caring way.

That's when I walked over to the nurse. I had gotten her ID before we left, so they would know who she was. "Here you go. This will tell you who she is. I think she's been here before," I said this with a hint of concern, but the tension in my voice was very noticeable.

The nurse wheeled her down the emergency room hallway into one of the small rooms. "OK, I'll look her up and get the doctor. You just wait here with her."

As the nurse said that to me, she lifted her up from the chair just as easily as I could. She lifted her up and set her right onto the bed.

I was waiting right by her side for fifteen minutes. I was waiting there holding her hand. She hadn't said or done anything except letting out a groan every once in a while. She had them all fooled again. She had them fooled, but I knew what she was doing. I knew it, and I had some hope because I knew they wouldn't give her anymore drugs.

That's when this really tall guy walked in the room. He was in hospital scrubs, so I thought he was the doctor. He leaned over to Jessica and asked, "How's it going there?"

"Huh? What?"

"I'm the doctor on staff today. I was told you are in a lot of pain."

"Yes, yes, I am."

"Well, we looked up your name in our computers, and unfortunately we can't give you any morphine. We see that you're on a list that prohibits us from giving you anything."

"I'm in pain! I really am. I am…."

"Well, it seems like you really are."

When the doctor said that I got really nervous. "You better obey the law." I said in an intense mutter.

I was really getting angry. I was getting angry again, but then I just realized that I needed to put my feelings aside and try and be there for her. I needed to try and help her get sober.

"I'm going to give you Baclofen. It's not an opiate so it is OK. It is a barbiturate. I'm going have the nurse give you an injection, and then write you a prescription for the same thing."

They were looking at her with concern. They were looking at her, and she had her eyes closed as though she was in pain. I walked over the chair that was in the corner, sat down, and put my head in my hands.

"Barbiturates are narcotics too" were the words racing through my mind.

I was going crazy because I wanted to tell them everything. I wanted to, but I had no ability to. I was helpless. I was completely helpless.

I felt my pulse go up as they were giving her the injection. It seemed at this point that it would never end. I didn't know what to do next. I had no idea. People had been giving me advice, but I had no ability to walk away from her.

After they gave her the injection, anyone could see that she was relaxed. It was as though she passed right out. She passed out, and I was waiting with her by her side until she woke up. Then I knew I was going to take her to the pharmacy in a cab, with a voucher, to get another drug filled.

"What am I going to do now?" I muttered as I started to cry.

Chapter 28: I Don't Know What To Do

It had been too much from the first visit I went with her to the emergency room, but this was really crazy. I thought that now she was on that federal list that it would solve everything. I had never seen anyone be as good at manipulating people, especially doctors. My mind was going out of control. I needed someone to talk to. I didn't want to talk to Chris because I had talked to him about her over and over. I knew that he was going to tell me that I needed to detach from her and to try an Al-Anon meeting. I needed help, so I thought that I would call James.

James had to at least be in his sixties. He had over thirty years of sobriety. Everyone in AA in San Francisco looked up to James. He was an older guy who was really skinny, always wore a hat, had a cane because he was legally blind, and was very soft spoken. But every time I talked to him, or heard him share from the podium or floor in an AA meeting, I knew that it was a solution. I needed help, and he was one of the few people that always accepted me at my worst. He was amazing. He seemed to genuinely love everyone, and everyone that I knew in AA loved him.

I picked up my cell phone and dialed the number. His phone rang once and then an answering machine answered, "Hello this is J—" Then he picked up the phone. "Hello," said James.

"Hey, James, it is me, Justin."

"Hey Justin, what's going on? You only seem to call me when you're going through it. So what's up?" He said all of this in a very jolly tone.

I could tell he wasn't being demeaning with that answer. He is just someone who always spoke the truth. That was one of the main things I loved about him. I knew he would be completely honest with me.

"Well I don't even know where to begin," I said.

"What do you mean? It must be really bad this time."

"Yes, it is. I feel hopeless. I told you I broke up with Brittany. You know that, don't you?"

"Yes. That was a good thing. That girl was soooooo crazy," he said this kind of laughing.

"Well, I went from one crazy relationship to another. It's maddening," I said.

"Tell me about it. What's so crazy about this one?"

"Well, I met her in a meeting, so I thought that she wanted to get sober. I thought that we'd be happy. She seemed so cool and loving. Now I don't know what to do."

"That really didn't tell me anything. I think you need to start from the beginning. So you're saying this is someone in recovery?"

"Yup. She's an addict. She's an addict who doesn't want to get sober. She scores all her dope in the emergency room. It is crazy because I know that she's lying to me about being in pain, but I can't stop helping her get these drugs. I want her to get sober. I want us to be happy."

"So you've been helping someone get dope in the emergency room while you are staying clean?"

I felt stupid and humiliated, but I just told him the truth. "Yup," I replied in a mopey tone. "She's an opiate and benzo addict who is scared of getting drugs on the street. She is the most amazing actress that I've ever met. She is so believable. She fools every doctor that she meets. She tells me she's in pain. I was believing her at first, and I'm not one of those crazy people in AA that says that you can't be on medication. Hell, I'm on medication! I believe that people can use medications if it is medically necessary. But she's just making it up! I don't know why, but I can't do anything except for what she wants. Even when I know it is wrong. You won't believe this."

"What's that?"

"They caught her. They found out she was lying. Her therapist even told me she was abusing the emergency rooms. She told her she couldn't work with her anymore. Her therapist told her that she was on a federal list now; if she shows up in an emergency room, they will refuse her. I felt safe because I thought that this would be the end. I thought that they wouldn't give her anything anymore, but I took her to the hospital again because she asked me to. I didn't want to, but I couldn't say no, and I thought that they wouldn't give her anything because she is on that federal list that tells the staff in the emergency rooms not to give any drugs to her. I still saw her talk the doctor into giving her drugs! This is CRAZY!" I was so angry it screamed the last word. I felt completely hopeless now.

With that James responded, "Justin, you are just as powerless over another person as you are over your own addiction. This was something that was difficult for me to grasp too, but we are all powerless over everything, in my opinion."

"What do you mean?"

"What I'm saying is that I really don't believe in free will."

"Well, neither do I. I see too much cause and effect everywhere."

"The reason I don't is that every action that I've taken in my life has been based on the pleasure principle. The pleasure principle is an ancient concept from Hinduism."

"That one makes sense to me too." Then I continued, "I don't know. It was just something that happened. I mean almost every male in my family is an alcoholic, so I guess it was just what was meant to be. Is this what you mean?"

"Kinda, but like is says in the Big Book, 'we find the feeling so elusive.' Do you remember that part?"

"Yup."

"Think of it this way, and this is just my take. Some people in AA don't agree with anything I say, but all words are open to interpretation. What I'm saying is that the reason why you drank is because it felt wonderful. It was probably the only thing that felt good to you. You found the feeling so amazing that it made you drink. It was the pleasure of drugs and alcohol that got you to drink and get high. This is why you were powerless over it all. It was this pleasure that was controlling you. You have been through a lot more than most people, Justin. I've heard your story, and it took all of that pain that you went through to seek a different solution. Alcohol was your only solution for the pain you were having for a long time because it gave you that pleasure, but now it gives you nothing but pain. It wasn't until you got in all that pain that you were able to seek relief. That relief cured you of the need to seek pleasure and gave you happiness. This is what recovery is all about. The only reason that you have recovery is that you got in enough pain. It took you a lot of pain to quit, didn't it?"

"A hell of a lot." I said this with a bit of confusion. I didn't know what he was going to say next, but I knew I needed to hear everything that he was telling me.

"You chased that pleasure until the pain was too unbearable. Now you have a different type of pain. A pain that is about a different type of powerlessness. This time you are starting to realize that you are powerless over another person. Think about it. You have been trying to get another person sober. What you're trying to do is that you are trying to control the uncontrollable. To me, all of the conflict in the world is about trying to control the uncontrollable, and most people don't realize that they don't have any control."

"My sponsor was telling me this the other day. So, then what am I supposed to do? I mean, I can see that things are determined, but how am I supposed to live without taking responsibility for my actions?"

"You do need to take responsibility for them."

"How can I do that if I don't have choices in anything I do?"

"I explain most things in paradoxes. It is just my way of looking at the world. I know that everything is determined in my heart, but I live as though I have free will. This is what makes it so I can truly comprehend my powerlessness over everything, and that I respond to pain. That, and it helps me to realize that I definitely have no control over other people. Hasn't this been proven to you?"

"It sure as hell has, but what am I supposed to do?"

"You need to comprehend that she is powerless over drugs, and you are powerless over her. You will continue to suffer as long as you try and control the uncontrollable. You need to experience the pain in order to grow; just like it says in the Big Book, 'pain is the touchstone of spiritual progress.' This is what it means to me. You have to have awareness over your pain and seek a solution."

"I know I'm in pain, but what am I supposed to do now?"

"I would recommend detaching and going to an Al-Anon meeting."

"But that's meant to deal with people like me! How can I go there?"

"I have been told, and I take this as true, that beneath every alcoholic is a codependent. I think everyone in the world has problems with other people, and most people in the world can't comprehend that they can't control the uncontrollable. Look at how much conflict there is in the world. Think of all of the difficulties and friction that come out of people trying to force the will that they truly don't have. This is where all difficulties humans have with each other arise from. You, and everyone else in the world, could use an Al-Anon meeting. I mean everyone. We are in societies. We all have problems with other people, and drugs are everywhere in America anyway."

This was making sense to me, but I didn't think I could bring myself to go to an Al-Anon meeting, so I responded, "I can't, I just can't. I mean it all make sense, and I can see the powerlessness over everything. I know I truly am. The only time that I gave up alcohol is when I just couldn't take it anymore. It was admitting that powerlessness over alcohol that got me to quit. It was like the only power I've ever gotten was admitting my powerlessness."

"Remember how it says that selfishness and self-centeredness, that we think is the root of our problem. It's not just you. Mankind as a whole is selfish and self-centered. This is what causes all the problems in the world. You are being selfish because you're trying to force a solution on her. A solution that she doesn't want. This isn't about her, this is about you. You have a desire to be happy. You think that another person will make you happy, just like you thought alcohol and drugs would make you happy. The conflict is that everyone wants to be happy and get what they desire. Most people just can't see that those desires lead to all kinds of problems, and do you know what?"

"What's that?"

"She is thinking that she's doing what is right."

"How could anyone think that that would be the right thing to do!"

"Most people get confused about what is right and what is justified. Think about it. I've seen the way you talk to people sometimes. Hell, I've never met anyone with your mouth." As he said this he stared to laugh. "You just justify it. You justify your behavior just like she is justifying hers. There is an ancient saying."

"What's that?"

"No one is willingly wicked. Haven't you heard that?"

"Yes."

"We all think that we're doing the next right thing. We seek pleasure and avoid pain, and the worst part is we all justify it. We live in ignorance, and the only way that we are brought out of that ignorance is by being put into enough pain. This is something that you are just going to have to experience. These are just my points of view, but you can come up with what is true for yourself."

"OK, I'll think about it, but it would just be easier if she did have something wrong with her! If she did get sick and die!" I screamed that, and as I did I felt really scared. I was scared that someone else knew that I thought that.

"See, Justin, you are being selfish. You would wish more pain on her, so you don't have to detach. You can't bring yourself to detach, and you feel that it would be easier for you if she suffered even more. Do you see how selfish that is?"

"Yup."

"Don't worry; I'm powerless over you too." With that he started to laugh again. "Just mull it over and do what you think is right. I have to get going now. I love you and take care."

"I love you too," I said.

We both hung up the phone. It was all so overwhelming. It made sense, but I just didn't—hell, I couldn't—believe that I couldn't help her. I was torn between wanting to help her and hating her. I felt as though she should be suffering with everything that she was putting me through. She should be suffering, but there was still a part of me that knew I could be happy with her. She just needed to stop the drugs. She needed to, and I could help her.

Chapter 29: A Sociopath

I had thought about everything James told me, but I didn't think I could go to Al-Anon. I didn't want to give up on Jessica. In fact, I wanted to see her. I had a feeling in me that if I headed over there we would be able to straighten some things out. She loved me, and I loved her.

After I hung up the phone with James, I walked down to the Stockton Tunnel. I was going to grab either the 30 or the 45 bus.

The driver stopped right where I was standing, so I was the first person on. There were only three seats left in the handicapped area. The rest of the bus was full, and it was going to get really packed with all the people at the next stop.

Right as I sat down, there was this older white guy who came right up behind me, "Hey, young man?"

I knew what he was going to say. I knew he was going to ask me for my seat, then I would have to explain my seizures to him. I also knew he either wouldn't understand, or just wouldn't believe me. I pulled out my disability pass and showed him.

I responded before he could say anything else. "I'm an epileptic, and I have seizures every day. That's why I'm sitting here, but there are two other seats that you can have. They're right over there." I pointed to two seats that were still open in the disabled and senior seating area.

"I don't want those! I want that one! You need to give me that one!"

I knew what Jessica had told me, so I was going to see if I could just put on my headphones and ignore him. Hell, I could remember what Chris and James were telling me as well. So I was just going to let a grumpy old man be a grumpy old man.

I put my headphones on and just tried to ignore him the whole way. It was crazy! He refused to sit in either of the other seats. They were open. I couldn't hear him, but I could tell that he wouldn't stop trying to bitch me out. I was now really starting to get angry. I couldn't take it too much longer, but my stop was coming right up. It was the second stop after the tunnel.

I pulled the leaver for the bus to stop. As I was getting up I said, "Excuse me."

I said it very politely to the old man because he was standing right in my way. I wasn't going to let him get to me.

He started to follow me to the bus's exit and tapped me on the shoulder. I turned off my headphones and he said, "Hey listen! I'm a senior! You should have gotten up for me! Life is too short to be treating people the way you do!"

I truly couldn't take it anymore! I tried to let it go from the beginning, but this was too much! So, I responded, "Well, yours is going to be over soon, so please leave me alone," I said this very calmly to prove to him that he didn't bother me in anyway.

With that, I hopped off the bus and headed up the hill to Jessica's place. I was muttering to myself the whole way, "I tried. I truly tried, but what was I supposed to do? Well, at least Jessica wasn't there."

I pounded my way up the steep hill to her apartment. It was getting a little late, but the sun was still out. I unlocked the gate. As I unlocked the gate I could hear some screaming upstairs. My throat clenched. I didn't want anything else crazy to happen, but I knew it was going to be.

I could hear some things crashing on the walls of the apartment. I ran up to the top of the steps. As I got up to the top of the stairs I saw Theo, so I asked him, "What's going on?" I said this in panic.

"Oh, it's just the usual." He said this as though there wasn't much happening while Jessica was screaming.

She was wailing, "Why did he say that about me! Why! I didn't do anything!"

"What's going on?" I asked again, looking at Theo. I didn't think I could talk to Jessica because she seemed so hysterical.

"It's nothing new," he said in a calm tone. "She's just upset because that guy that she broke up with to go out with you is calling her on what she does to people.'"

"What do you mean? I don't understand?" I replied.

"He said I was a sociopath! Why did he say this? I just want to die! I want to die!" She was screaming as loud as she could.

I was really confused. She ran right into her room and I followed her. "Let me call 911!" I said in a deep panic.

Theo responded with a laugh, "Why? She's always like this. I have been dealing with this for the last twenty years. There's nothing to worry about. I mean if she did have all of those medical issues she has lied to you about she'd be dead by now. She's just crazy. That's all she is. Justin, this is nothing new." He continued to laugh.

I was in shock because he seemed too calm as she was yelling over and over. It wasn't even words, just wailing. I looked on the ground next to her bed and I saw the empty bottle of pills that the doctor in the emergency room prescribed. I didn't know what to do next.

She fell to the ground. She was on her hands and knees, and she wouldn't stop screaming, "I'm a sociopath! I'm a sociopath!"

Wham! Wham! Wham! She slammed her head against the dresser that was right next to her bed. She was pounding her head as hard as she could! She wouldn't stop! Now she was just screaming and yelping without any words!

I whipped out my cell phone to dial 911. It started to ring. "911, what's your emergency?" the operator answered.

That's when she leaped up and grabbed the phone out of my hand. "Don't do that! I'm not going to the psych ward! I just want to die! You need to let me die! He said I was a sociopath!" She grabbed the phone out of my hand and hung up on the operator.

My mind was swarming. I didn't know what to do, so I just grabbed her and held onto her. I didn't let her go. I just started to hug her. "Hey," I said gently, "Calm down. I'm right here. It will be OK. Don't worry about it. You're not a sociopath. Just relax. It will be OK. It will, I promise."

"The only way it will be OK is if she does kill herself, but that won't happen. She been yelling that to me for years now." After Theo said that he just turned and walked out of the room. "I'll let you take it from here." With that I heard him close the door to his own room.

I didn't do anything except to hold her. I was holding her and stroking her head. "It's going to be OK. I love you, OK. You're not a sociopath. It will be OK."

I didn't know if it was going to be OK or not; in fact, I didn't think it was. I was feeling like it was never going to be OK, but I couldn't let her know that. I could never be anything except what she needed me to be.

She only came up to my breast, so I had one arm around her. My other arm was stroking the back of her head. I glanced back down at the bottle. It was tipped over completely so I knew it was empty.

"Anyone who can lie like this just might be a sociopath. She doesn't seem to care what she says to anyone as long as she gets her drugs." I thought that I was filled with resentment.

She was staring to relax. She tried talking but nothing came out except slurring. The whole bottle of pills had taken complete effect.

I laid her down on the bed, then I laid down with her. She started to snore pretty quickly. She was asleep, but my mind was spinning. I went from compassion to anger. I couldn't believe that I was the one showing up for her over and over! No matter what, it felt like it was never going to end! Why couldn't she be there for me at least one time! I am always the one that is trying to solve her problems!

She was only in her bra and underwear anyway, so I just pulled the blankets over her. That's when I realized that I didn't have any medication. I hadn't, and I didn't care; in fact, I was going to make sure that night that I wouldn't take my medication! She was going to have to show up for me! It was always about her! It was about time that she showed up for me!

I was boiling with rage, and after a while, because I didn't have any medication, I was getting more and more energy. I could feel the mania staring to come on. The anger turned into energy in my brain. It started to feel great. This time when she woke up, she was going to have to take me to the hospital!

Chapter 30: Pigs Fly and Have Wings

All of her pictures of Grace Kelly were pointing their eyes directly toward me. I was getting more and more energy as my legs and feet were starting to shake. She was fast asleep and snoring. I knew she was completely passed out because she would only snore when she was really loaded on drugs.

It had been several hours, but time was moving faster and faster. It was the euphoria from my mania that was starting to lift me from this bed to a place where only I could go. I knew I would have my mind only for a couple more hours. I truly didn't care because I had started to feel high. This high was what fueled by my resentment of always being there for her. I was always there for her, and she was never there for me. This time was going to be different.

As my lower body was shaking, I was holding her with my arms, and they remained steady and calm. All of Grace's eyes were getting too much for me. The problem was that when I shut my eyes, the splotches that were reflected back to me from my eyelids were turning into faces. They were more like skulls with tongues that were swirling around in their mouths.

"Boo!" they shouted to me.

I could read their lips but no sound came out of their mouths. Every time that happened, it scared my eyes open, but then Grace's glare would overwhelm me so I shut my eyes again. The lights were completely off in the room, but the little amount of light that came through the bedroom window was enough to fuel all of the demons.

I had started to breathe quickly and heavily. The air had numbed my face. Before I had realized it, I felt the sun starting to rise. I could tell that it had become early morning, but the rays of light felt like they were hitting me in the middle of summer on a tropical island because of the sweat that covered my body. I still had the wits to realize that this was San Francisco, so it never got too hot, but the energy was just enhancing my madness. I knew it was madness, and I knew where I was going, but I didn't care because she had driven me to insanity every time with her selfish behavior.

There was a feather in the cap of one of the many Grace pictures on the wall, and with the sun rising it started to slowly turn into a fly around the room. I was more scared of the drops of shit that were going to start littering the room, so with the fear of the rodent from the sky I closed my eyes. But as soon as I closed my eyes, the splotches turned into crazier faces again and would startle me back to the disturbed consciousness of the moment.

I was really starting to get frightened. After a little while longer I didn't know if I truly wanted to go through with this, but my resentment kept me willing in the most perverted way. I was crazy for putting up with her; I knew that. Then I was going crazy just to drive her crazy. It was revenge!

She snorted and sniffled a little more; with that, I lifted my left arm up to look at the time. It didn't even seem to cross my mind about what time it was until now; 9:23 a.m. is what it said on my watch. I reached my hand up in the air to touch the ceiling, and then I saw traces and shadows start to follow my arm's movements. After looking at my watch I wanted to see if she had slept off most of her high.

"Hey, Jessica, Jessica, wake up. Wake up!" I screamed the second time.

"Ah! What, what are you doing?" She woke startled and screamed out the "ah," but then the rest of the words slowed down to a groggy slurring response.

"Hey!" I shouted really quickly. "Hey! I don't know if you remember last night? But you were going crazy, so I laid you down and held you all night." I was starting to talk faster and faster because my mania was really starting to kick in.

"What's going on? Why are you talking so quickly?"

"Well, I haven't had my meds. I was taking care of you all night, so now I'm starting to get manic. I'm also starting to hallucinate!"

"What? What do you mean? Why didn't you take your medication?"

"Couldn't! I was busy taking care of you!"

"Slow down! Would you please slow down? I can't even think as quickly as you are talking!"

"I'm also going to start having seizures too. If I go too long without them, I might even have a big one!"

"What?" she screamed. "Let's get you back to your place so we can get you your medication!"

"Too late! I probably need to go to the hospital! Oh see, watch my eyes! I'm starting to have a small seizure right now!"

"Slow down! Just slow down! I can't handle this!"

"Just watch!" I couldn't stop talking quickly. I had no power to, and as I stared directly into her eyes I was showing her that my pupils were oscillating.

"What!" She jumped right out of bed. She seemed to have a hard time standing up because she was still intoxicated. She was; I could tell she was. Even as I was starting to lose my mind and have seizures, I could tell she was still messed up from the drugs the night before. This was all staring to give me a perverse satisfaction. I could tell this was all wrong, but I was really loving it all. I was so pissed about how much I did for her. I did it over and over, and she was the one that was always lying to me. I was sick of bending over backwards for her. She was lying about all of it, and I knew it. I had known it for a long time. It was as though this was the only type of revenge I could ever get. It felt so good to cause her this trouble.

"Shit! I'm having another one!"

"Another what?"

"Seizure!"

"Would you slow down? I'm still fucked up!"

"What do you mean? Did you do any drugs last night?" I was playing ignorant because I just wanted to see her response.

"Well, um, I just took what was prescribed. Nothing more. Besides it doesn't matter. I need to get you to the hospital!"

I leaned back my head and let out a witches' cackle, "Ahahahah!" Then I had a loud snort.

"What's going on? Why didn't you go home to get your meds?" she asked with anger. "Come on!" she screamed as she jumped out of bed and then hit the floor.

Wham! "Ouch!" she cried as she tried to get up, but she was still a little wobbly.

With that I giggled even more. "Are you OK?" I asked.

I wanted her to think that I was really concerned, but inside I wanted her to panic. My high was getting bigger and bigger, and I knew that I would completely lose my mind in about an hour. I had been to a hospital so many times that it never bothered me. I had been locked up for months at a time, and even though I was starting to lose my mind, I knew that all they would do would be stabilize me and get me out the door. Thinking all of this made me laugh harder and harder, "Ahahaha!"

"Why are you laughing? This isn't funny! What am I supposed to do?"

"Sorry! I'm just laughing because I'm starting to get really manic! When I do I start feeling really high! I mean it's great, but I can't do it too often or else they'll never let me out of the hospital! Ahahaha!"

"Stop laughing! And slow down! Just slow down!"

"Sorry, don't think I can! Ahaha!"

She was trying to get dressed as fast as she could. I could tell she was having problems even as the colors were getting brighter and brighter in the room. The whole room was starting to move a little, and all the bright colors were moving together.

She was completely dressed, and I had had my clothes on all night. The only thing I needed to put on was my shoes. I hopped up really quickly, so quickly that it scared her even more, and she stumbled backwards. She was close to the wall so she reached out one hand and caught herself.

"Wow!" she said as she stabilized herself. "Come on! Do you have any money for a cab?"

"Not too sure!"

She reached around to my back pocket and I didn't even struggle. There was a part of me that wanted to go on the bus just to give her more trouble, but I was starting to get crazier and crazier. I had had lots of simple partial seizures, so I knew we should take a cab. I gave in and let her grab the money out of my wallet.

"Great!" she said, "You have $40 on you! Come on! Let me call one! What's the number for the cab company?"

She knew I had it memorized, so I just told her.

"Yes, can you get a cab to this apartment really quickly?" she asked them. She gave them the address, and then grabbed me by my hand and said, "Let's go! Come on!"

"OK, but I'm starting to have more and more seizures!"

"AH! Let's get out of here!" She pulled me all the way down the stairs. I thought she was about to fall down this flight as well because she had such a hangover.

She sat me down on the steps and closed the gate, and then she got out onto the street to wait for the cab. All of the cars on the street were starting to float in the air, just a couple of inches. As I saw that happening, I leaned my head back and started to laugh even more. It was all getting so amusing. She had deserved it!

The yellow cab pulled up and flashed its lights. "There he is! Come on, let's get you in there! Hurry!" she screamed, and as she screamed she tripped backward and hit the pavements. "Ouch! That hurt!"

I let out another cackle, "Rahahah!"

"Don't laugh! Get in the cab!"

I was able to help her up, and she opened the door to the cab with her skinned hands.

"Where to?" the diver asked calmly.

"Saint Francis Hospital! Hurry! I need to get him to the emergency room!"

"OK. Just relax. It's right over the hill."

"I know!" she screamed.

The cab started to drive away, and as it took off I rested my arm on the black leather of the car door. The black leather stared to turn a little green. It was getting rougher and rougher. It seemed to be turning to the texture of alligator skin. Now I was really starting to shift from humor to fear. The euphoria was turning into tension. I knew I was going to panic soon.

"Damn!" I screamed

"What! What is it?" she asked.

"I'm starting to have anxiety!" I didn't know what to do next. I felt the acceleration of the cab, so this told me we were getting closer to the hospital.

"We're here," the cab driver said calmly. "$6.60."

As she paid him she said, "Come on! Hurry up!"

I picked up my pace because I didn't want to have the panic attack. I was following her as fast as I could, as I was running around the obstacles that were popping up in my way.

"Someone help us!" she screamed as she got me in the automatic doors to the emergency room.

A nurse came running out. "What? What's going on? How can we help?"

"My boyfriend is an epileptic and bipolar, and he hasn't had his medication! He is starting to hallucinate and have seizures! He said he is even going to start having a panic attack!" she said all of this as she was holding my hand.

"Let's get him in here," the nurse responded. "Just calm down. We got it now."

The nurse pulled out a wheelchair and sat me down in it. She wheeled me down the hall, then got me up.

"Here, let's get your clothes off and get you into a gown. I'll get the doctor." She handed me the gown and went out of the room, down the hall.

I knew the routine from here. I got all of my clothes off except my boxers and slid the gown over my front side with the back held wide open. As I laid down on the gurney, the doctor walked into the room. I couldn't understand much because I had finally lost my mind. Everything was turning into a blur. That's when I saw some pink pigs that started to come out of the walls. They were accompanied by dollar signs. The pigs had white wings and started to fly around the room. I saw a gigantic syringe with an enormous needle which was stuck right into the vein in my left arm.

I leaned my head back and let out one last slow cackle, "Rahahahah!" With that my vision went black and the drug knocked me out.

Chapter 31: Truly Powerless

I was finally at home. I had just gotten back from the emergency room, and I truly didn't know what to think or do. She did show up for me. For the first time it was about me, and it made me feel terrible. I couldn't believe what I did to myself. I could have had brain damage from having a large seizure, and I could have been put in another psych ward for not taking my medication. They sent me home with a bottle of Lorazepam in case a had a large seizure. Jessica asked me if she could have it. I didn't know what else to do except give it to her.

She was at home now. I told her I needed to go home and get some rest, but I couldn't get any. There was no way that my mind would be quiet with what I just did, so I decided to use the tool that I have always been trained to use in recovery: the phone.

I dialed the number again. I knew what he was going to tell me, but I just need the clarity of a sane and sober mind. Mine was sober, but I could tell that after what I just did it wasn't sane.

The phone rang once and then the voicemail started, "Hello, this," then he picked up the phone and said, "Hello?"

"Hey, James. How's it going? It's Justin."

"Hey, Justin. What's going on this time?"

"I did the craziest thing. I am completely nuts. That's all I know. You told me I am powerless over another, and I wouldn't accept it. I wouldn't, and I did an extremely crazy thing. I guess I've done crazier, but not since I've gotten sober. Nothing this crazy." I said all of this in a very depressed tone.

"What did you do this time?" He started to laugh. "And I am sure you're right, you have done something crazier. I've known you awhile, so I've seen you do it all."

"Well it was nuts. I showed up to Jessica's apartment to spend the night with her, and she was high again. It was so crazy! She was blacked out on barbiturates that I helped her get from the emergency room. She was going crazy, and some guy she once dated was calling her a sociopath. So, she swallowed the whole bottle. It got really crazy because she was screaming and yelling. She even started slamming her head against the dresser."

"So, what was your reaction to it all? Did you try and solve a problem that you couldn't?"

"Yup. I calmed her down and got her into bed. She passed out, and that's when my insanity really hit me. I was really angry that I was always showing up for her. I was always showing up for her, and she just used me every time. She used me to get drugs, and I always just went along with it—all because I couldn't say no. That alone was crazy, but that wasn't even the craziest thing that I did."

"So, what else did you do?"

"Well I, I mean, well, I stayed with her all night. She was passed out, so I decided to just hold her all night. Then it dawned on me that I hadn't taken my medication. I knew that if I didn't, I would end up in the hospital. I knew I would have seizures and hallucinate, but I did it anyway because I was sick of always being there for her. I wanted her to be there for me."

"What else happened? Did you end up in the hospital?"

"It was nuts. I was hallucinating, having seizures, and getting manic. I also almost had a panic attack, but I didn't care. I wanted her to feel what I was always going through for her. I wanted her to have to be there for me. I didn't care about my life. I just wanted her to feel what it was like, so yes, I wound up in the hospital." I said all of this as I was staring to cry. "I'm a lunatic! I have to be! Who else would do that! After I got out they gave me a prescription so I wouldn't have a large seizure. They gave it to me, but then she asked me for it, so I couldn't do anything except give it to her."

"Yes, Justin, that does seem like insanity. I have told you this before. You are powerless. I have a question for you?"

"What's that?" I started to get a little nervous.

"Will you take a suggestion if I give it to you? I mean if you don't, it's cool. You're the one that is suffering."

"Yes, I know I am. It's never been so obvious to me that I put myself through this, and It is driving me crazy."

"Can you admit that you are not just powerless over alcohol, but you are also powerless over another human being?"

"Well, I feel powerless. I feel powerless over the whole world, but what do you mean about everything?"

"It says in the Big Book that pain is the touchstone of spiritual progress."

"I know."

"Well, it means to me that I have to be beaten into a state of reasonableness. We all do. Don't worry, it's not just you. It's everyone. This is what the pleasure principle is about."

"You talked with me about this last time."

"Yup, and the only way we change is when we get in enough pain. It's not just you, it's everyone. The whole world does this. This is why it is such a main part of all of the eastern religions. This was thought of in the oldest spiritual texts that there are; but something I do is that I pray for a lower tolerance of pain because it is the only reason I change for the better. Justin, you have had a very high tolerance of pain your whole life. I've heard your story, and I saw you walk in and out of AA for years. It wasn't until you got in enough pain that you finally quit drinking and doing drugs. Now you have to accept the fact that you have no control over other people. Another line in the Big Book is: 'we cease fighting everyone and everything.' This is what it truly means to be powerless and what it truly means to surrender."

"But I want love. Isn't that worth trying for?"

"You can have love. You can have all the love you want. Why don't you just try giving it to everyone instead of someone that is unavailable? If you really loved her, you would just accept her and realize that you can't control her. You can't get her to be the person that you want her to be. That's not love, that's selfishness. You need to detach. You need to love her by letting her find her path. You are only prolonging her usage. You've been helping her get the drugs. You gave her a medication they gave to you to save your life, and you gave it to her because you couldn't say no to her. You are powerless. I don't think you can get any crazier than that when it comes to an intimate relationship. Well maybe you can if you are also going to put your life at risk."

"I don't know why I can't! There is just something inside me that can't walk away! I don't know why! I was wishing she would get sick and die! It would be so much easier than me having to walk away! She has been telling me this whole time that she is sick! Why can't she be sick!" I was screaming and crying this.

"The reason why is that you want what we all want. You want love. If you want it, you're getting it from me. You've gotten it from all kinds of people in recovery. You need to find someone that wants to live in a solution. You're not showing her love. You are being selfish. If you would rather her dead, then you walk away; that is just a self-centered fear. Remember what it says in the Big Book: 'fear that we will either lose something that we already have, or fail to get something that we demand.' That is what causes all our fears, and all our problems. Every person's problems. You can find love. It is out there, and you can have love for her. You just need to realize that you have to detach because what you're doing isn't love. It is selfishness. If you try an Al-anon meeting it will help you love all kinds of people. It will help you participate in the relationships that will be good for you."

"I can't detach! I don't know why, but it feels just like when I couldn't quit drinking! I mean I did everything that my sponsors always told me! I have one that said every time you feel like drinking to give me a call! I called him every time, but I always went out drinking! This feels just like the same thing! I can't control myself!"

"You need to realize that you can stop your suffering anytime that you want. The most loving thing you could do for her is to detach and let her have the consequences that she needs to experience in this life time. She will never get sober unless she feels those consequences. You are making the situation worse for yourself and her. Let go, let go for her and yourself. Why don't you try going to an Al-Anon meeting tonight? Just see what happens and if they have anything to offer you. They are all over the city, and there are lots of double winners."

"Double winners?"

"People that are both in AA and Al-Anon. I think everyone can use an Al-Anon meeting, everyone in the whole world. This isn't something that you alone have gone through. There are lots of people. Why don't you go? Why don't you just text her? Don't call, just text. You can tell her you love her in that text, and you can tell her that that means you need to find separate paths. You need to understand that you are making both her life and yours worse by being in this relationship. Can I tell you one more thing?"

"What's that?"

"You are a very loving person. I've seen it. You have been trying to love her. It is just that you are confused with what love is. Like I told you, love to me is wanting the best for someone and taking the necessary steps to carry that out. If you love her, you will detach. Your problem is that you only try to love a certain few, but if you want love, try giving it to everyone. Try not to go off on people and degrade them. Try to show everyone the same patience that you chose to only show a select few. I can tell why you are so hostile to people."

"Why's that?" I asked nervously.

"You are a very scared person. You are frightened of people. You want them all to love you, but you don't want to be vulnerable. You don't let anyone near you accept for a select few. If you let down your guard and try to love everyone, you'll realize that it is just a fear. A fear that you don't need to participate in. I have had lots of fear, and fear of people was one of the main ones. It is for all of us. That's why it's in the Promises. Do you know what that fear is?"

"No."

"It is a fear of not knowing. You don't know, and you can't read others' minds, so you expect the worst. We all have a fear of not knowing. We've all felt judged by others. We all want all the answers. The whole point is that none of us will ever get the answers except God. God is available to anyone, and He is available to you too."

"That makes sense, but I've just never tried to apply it to another person."

"The point that we all have the fear of not knowing. We all want the answers. Pride tells us that we have the answers, but the only answer is that we don't know a damn thing. We have to accept that we are powerless over everything. Sure, we can know God. He is available to anyone, and God is the only truth. But God is something that has to be sought. There is a line in the Bible that I like a lot: 'things long sought are often more cherished.' You want love, and you need God as well. That's what God is: love. It is within all of us. But everything else, if you take it as fact or a guess, will just lead to fear. So why don't you text her, and then go to a meeting? OK?"

"I'll go, but I still don't know if I can detach."

"Have it your way. I can't tell you what to do, and I'm not going to try. Well, Justin, I love you. That's why I'm taking my time, and you can love anyone. That should be your goal. If you want love, just try giving it to everyone. Have a good night."

"Bye."

We both hung up the phone, then I turned on my laptop and began to search for an Al-Anon meeting I could go to. I couldn't believe that it came to this. I was crying and nervous as hell because I knew he was right. I knew I needed to go.

Chapter 32: A True Surrender

I had seen that there was an Al-Anon meeting at 6 p.m. over on Church Street. It was the same building that I went to for my morning meeting. I saw it was at 6, so I waited till about 6:05. I didn't want to have to talk to anyone beforehand. I didn't know what to expect, but now I was willing to try what James recommended. Hell, what else could I do? It was obvious that I was powerless, I just didn't think that I would ever be able to detach.

When I got into the room, I was surprised to see who was at the front of the room. It was this guy Jessie that was speaking. I knew him from AA. In fact, I saw a couple of different people in the room from AA. My heart was a little nervous, but when I saw the other people I recognized, I felt a little better. I guess they were double winners as well.

They read all of the readings. The readings were all different from AA, except the steps. The steps were very similar, with minor adjustments to fit people who suffered from another's drinking or drug use; in fact, Step One was exactly the same. It was about being powerless over alcohol.

When all of the readings were finished, the secretary said, "Now, let's go around the room and introduce ourselves." Some AA meetings do that, but not all of them.

In AA, when people introduce themselves they give their name and then say that they are an alcoholic, then everyone in the room would respond. Here people were just introducing themselves by their first name. It went very quickly because the only thing anyone said was their name and no one responded.

Then the secretary said, "Now, we ask if there are any newcomers that would like to introduce themselves by their first name only; we do this not to embarrass you, but so that we may get a chance to get to know you. Do we have any new members, either to Al-Anon, or to this meeting?"

I said, "My name is Justin."

"Hi, Justin" was the group's response.

A couple of others introduced themselves as well. Then the secretary said, "Now it is time for the speaker to share his experience, strength, and hope. Here is Jessie."

I had heard Jessie speak a lot in AA, and I really enjoyed everything he had to say. He was a really smart guy. Jessie was a white guy from the South. He had long hair and was wearing a white t-shirt with grey jeans. He always seemed to dress that way.

"My name is Jessie," he said.

"Hi Jessie," the group responded.

"What I'm going to talk about today is Step One and Eleven. When I got here I was in a desperate state of mind. I had been sober for 23 years in AA, but when it came to other people I was just as powerless over them as I was over alcohol. I had come because I was in a relationship with this guy. He was currently using speed. I wanted monogamy, but he was always going out and cheating on me. I found that in the end I was following him around trying to make sure that he behaved and kept his word. His drug usage was getting worse, and I couldn't walk away. I haven't really ever met any monogamous crystal addicts, so that was another part of my insanity."

Everyone laughed.

Jessie continued, "When I got here I had been following him for days. I even ended up pounding on his door in the middle of the night screaming: 'I know you're in there!' He was in there, and he was with another man. It was as though I was foaming at the mouth with my anger, and when I took a step back, I saw how angry I gotten in that moment. It finally made me take a look at myself. I was amazed with how much control I had lost. I wanted control. I wanted him to be the way I felt he should be. This to me was the only way I could be happy. The insanity was that I was having expectations for someone who wasn't available.

"I thought it was all about love. Love was what I wanted, but at that moment it was as though I finally saw all of my anger and fear. It came up and hit me in the face. I had driven myself crazy by engaging with this man: Someone that I wanted to love me, but it was my unreasonable expectations that drove me to my madness. I have heard it said in these rooms that expectations are resentments that are waiting to happen, and I had the expectation that we had the same values.

Values are what everyone in the whole world fights over. Every war is about people expecting other people to have their values. When they don't, they can't accept it, and then the answer is violence and chaos. Him not sharing my values meant that I had gotten really angry, and it was my anger that was controlling me. I was completely powerless, and it wasn't until I walked into my first Al-Anon meeting that I realized I couldn't control him or me, and I shouldn't expect him to value what I value. I was the one being controlled by my motivations.

Everyone is controlled by their motivations. This is something that pertains to more than just people who are affected by the disease of alcoholism. I would say one of the problems with people in recovery is that they all think that they are too unique. A lot of people in recovery think that they are the only ones that seek pleasure to the point of insanity. Everyone has their addictions in one way or another. People eat too much. There are those that crave money to the point where it hurts themselves and others. Sex addiction is another one. People gamble and lose everything. The list goes on. In the east, it is selfish desires that control us and lead to all our problems. My selfish desire at that moment was for him to value what I valued. Remember, even though you can choose your own higher power in recovery, all our literature is still based on Christianity, and all religions have a lot in common.

"All religions talk about how there is something wrong with human nature, and they all give ways to fix it. With my higher power, it has shown me that my problem is that I'm blind to my motivations, which are my selfish desires. When we are blind to our motivations, we are truly powerless. I believe we all have two core motivations: fear and love. The problem is we get confused on which one is which. You would think that it would be easy to feel fear, and to know what love is as well.

People have been trying to give a good definition of love all throughout human history. Everyone agrees that love exists, but there are lots of different definitions and conclusions that people get to. I would also say that some are confused about what love is. We all know love is in each of us, but what truly is it?

I had someone I looked up to once tell me that love is wanting the best for someone and taking the necessary steps to carry that out. This is a definition I got from someone I looked up to in Al-Anon. This is something that has been very helpful for me to contemplate. For one, I thought I knew what was best for people. I had no ability to see that when I think I know something, it is usually just an opinion. All I pretty much have are my opinions because there are really only two things that I can know for sure: God and myself. I got this from the eastern point of view as well, and it makes a lot of sense to me.

I do believe that God is love, and when I truly love God, I love myself, and the best way to love God and myself is to show love to others. The only way I have found myself able to have compassion for myself was learning how to have compassion for others. There is a big difference in knowing what is right for someone, and just loving and accepting them. This means the decisions others make are beyond my control.

Some people say that 12-step programs are selfish because we are here to take care of ourselves. We see that we have driven ourselves to chaos, or put other's needs before ours, and all the problems that this behavior has caused us. I disagree with 12-step programs being selfish. I would say they are about self-abandonment. This is about being selfless, and when I am truly selfless is when I do the best thing for myself and others.

We have more in common with each other than we like to think. All our differences are cosmetic. Everyone has that perfect soul that it talks about in all religions, and it is that perfect soul that I have that is identical to everyone else's. It all has to do with God, and what truly is, is what is perfect. I have spent most of my life focusing on how unique I was. This is where I use to get all of my importance. It wasn't until I could accept that I was just like everyone else that I finally felt comfortable with myself. When I could love them, I could love myself.

Like it says in the literature, we are driven by one-hundred forms of self, and this is the cause of all our problems. When I see people as different, and I expect them to have my values, that is selfishness. When I give up those expectations, and do what God would have me do for myself and others, as well as see how we have that perfect soul, that is self-abandonment.

God's will is another thing that people try to define, and I would say that a lot of people are very confused about what God's will is as well. Some believe that God's will is something that they should force on other people. They have their doctrine and dogma that tells them what God is for them and other people. God's will is only a solution that the individual should apply to the themselves.

When I think I know what God's will is for another, that isn't God's will. That would be ego, and ego is pride, which is fundamentalism. This is why fundamentalism is contrary to God's will. When I think I know what God's will is for another, that is another way I am forcing my values on that person, and that is me playing God. It is nothing but selfishness to tell another what God's will is, and to me, and every spiritual doctrine that I have read, God's will is about being selfless.

The most selfless thing to do when it comes to others is to accept them. I need to accept everyone, including the alcoholics in my life, because when it comes down to it, I don't know what is best for them. I really don't feel as though I know what is best for me most of the time. God is the only one that knows what is best for each of us, and that's why I have purpose in my life today.

My purpose is that everything I go through is for a reason, and that reason is to grow to be a better person. Blind faith is about believing in something I can't prove. The literature tells us not to have blind faith. Faith to me isn't about believing in something I can't prove. I use faith to see through my clouded mind. It is a light in my darkness. Faith is about my life having purpose in every experience that I have and every action that I take, and being at peace with not knowing. It is about acknowledging that there is a purpose with everything that everyone goes through.

I was a very cynical person when I got here. A lot of my life was about how victimized I was. I always wanted what I wanted, and I had no ability to see that there was a plan for me which was beyond my knowledge. Now I see that I just needed to learn things, and this is why I need to have awareness.

Awareness is one of the main concepts that has been brought to me by the 11th Step. This is one of the most important steps, in my opinion. The 11th Step, as most of you know, is about prayer and meditation. Like it says, prayer and meditation is something that needs to be practiced. When these steps were written, I'm sure they didn't have the concept of the eastern meditations that I do, but I find it the most rewarding. It is all about staying in the moment and having complete control over my mind. When I'm in the moment, I get to be aware of my motivations instead of being completely controlled by them. I get to ask myself: do I want to live out of fear, or do I want to live out of love? The answer to that is that I always want to live out of love. So, the truly next right action is brought about by the clarity of awareness. Who would willingly want to be in a fear based state of mind? This is the problem that I see all over the world.

It is in the news every day with all of the tragic things that happen. I would say that most people are controlled by at least some level of fear, and they are blind to that control as well. My goal is to be completely free of fear, so I can always take the right action. Being able to take the right action in every situation is what I call absolute awareness. Absolute awareness is something I know I will most likely never get completely, but it is something I should always strive for. When it comes to this fear that is controlling my life, it says in the literature, fear is just a boogeyman. I don't need to be consumed with it like I was when I was pounding on his door. I can respect it when someone takes a different path than the one my mind tells me and them we should take; because if I truly love someone, I will do nothing but accept them.

What I have always wanted from the world was acceptance. I grew up in an alcoholic household, so I didn't get it from anyone in my family. I always felt judged. I took that behavior that I learned from those sick people, sick people that I know today were doing their best, the only thing that they knew how to do, and I passed that judgement on to others. People can only do what they know, and what they know was what was done to them. It was this judgment that was my problem, and it was my judgment. My judgment was based on fear, and whenever I am aware of that fear today I get to make the best decision for myself, no one else, and turn away from it to a solution that works for me today. This is all something that I learned from, so it has a purpose today.

I am going to read my favorite prayer. This is a prayer that whenever I'm wondering what is the right thing to do, I look to the words in this prayer. It helps me make the best decision. It is the Prayer of Saint Francis. It goes:

> Lord, make me a channel of thy peace.
> Where there is hatred may I bring love,
> Where there is wrong I may bring the spirit of forgiveness,
> Where there is discord may I bring harmony,
> Where there is error may I bring truth,
> Where there is doubt may I bring faith,
> Where there is sadness may I bring joy,
> Where there are shadows may I bring light.
> Lord, grant that I may seek rather to comfort than to be comforted,
> To understand than to be understood,
> To love than to be loved.
> For it is by self-forgetting that one finds,
> It is by forgiving that one is forgiven,
> It is by dying that one awakens to eternal life.
> Amen.

"I could do without the amen and the eternal life part because I'm not a Christian."

Everyone laughed.

Jessie continued, "Prayer to me is not about getting my desires met. I've met a lot of people that say prayer doesn't work because they prayed for things and they didn't come true. I shouldn't pray that the alcoholic in my life does my will and has my values. Prayer isn't about 'grant me thy wishes' like it says in the Big Book. It is about being in the right state of mind so I can handle anything that comes my way. Prayer is about getting to that absolute awareness, so the solution is available to me no matter what I go through. If I am always in the solution, I can handle anything, and fear is nothing but a boogeyman.

"When I forgave that man for all of his behavior, I was able to see I had a lot to be forgiven for as well. I realized that we all do. Like a said I'm not a Christian, but to me original sin is a very good concept.

The only thing original sin means is that there is something corrupt about humans because of our ability to reason. There are lot of problems that humans have that aren't found in other life: greed, vengeance, craving more power, and a whole list of other things. Humans use the tool of intellect to the detriment of others. The atom bomb was only brought about by the mind's capacities. It took intelligence to come up with the commodity of money, and look at all the problems that come with that. So, original sin is a very logical concept. I would also say that original sin is the cause of the selfish desires.

"I was in college once, years ago, and I had this anthropology professor that wouldn't stop saying bad things about Christianity. Then one day he said, 'There was something corrupted about humans given our ability to reason.' That's when I told him it sounded like he was making the argument for original sin. I started to laugh, but he didn't find it funny at all. In fact, he got really angry. I have to be careful not to make people angry when they are controlling my grades."

Everyone laughed again.

"This means that the concept of original sin was true for him too. He just hated Christianity. But really, I hated God when I got to AA too, but since then I found something, and Al-Anon has only enhanced this connection.

"Words aren't good for God because it is beyond description. God is nothing I can understand with my mind. I have limited constructs of what God is, like love and something that has all the answers, but it is more of a nebulous construct for me. God is an experience that I have gotten. The only way anyone can truly understand God is through an experience, not a rational mind. The rational mind will lead to the experience, but the experience is the true answer that I got through things like meditation. I believe in different stages of reality. This physical world is the lowest, but it is also the gateway to what truly is, so I can't disregard it either. This is why I need to have faith and the ability to believe.

"I have found it beneficial to believe, and I explore all religions today. Since I have taken that leap of faith, it has showed me through that experience that God does exist. I once took all religions as stupid, but the more research that I have done, and the more I have opened my mind, then the better my solutions have gotten. Today I take them as all having truth. Some more than others, but they all speak to the same universal premises.

"It was God that got me to explore, and it wasn't until I truly started looking for a solution that my life opened up. It started with AA, but like they say, Al-Anon is graduate school. My goal today is to love everyone. My goal today is to be there and accept people instead of judging them. One of the things original sin got me to realize is that no matter who we are, we all have it. It doesn't mean that we are terrible people. It is just what is. If I can accept that in others, then I can accept it in myself. I should accept it in others, for I realized that a sinner shouldn't judge another sinner for sinning. That would be hypocrisy, and hypocrisy is a sin.

"The more I have accepted others, the more peaceful my state of mind has gotten. I am not perfect. I screw up all the time, but because of the steps I get to ask myself the question: do I want to live in fear? When I realize I don't, I ask myself, what I can do to straighten out my behavior? I will end with this: people say in recovery that it is progress, not perfection. I would say that today I have acceptance; and since I have acceptance, of myself and others, I strive for perfection, but I'm grateful for progress. I have perfect goals and ideals. I try to accept everyone because this is God's world, and nothing happens in God's world by mistake. When I want someone to be any other way than the way God made them, then I am saying that I know better than God. If I am saying I know better than God, all that is ego, and knowing God is about humility. When it comes to others, all I should do is love and accept them. It matters not what others do. It only matters what I do. It is this that gets me to continue to strive for these prefect goals and ideas which makes it so I never give up making progress.

"I leave perfection up to God, and the paradox is that I am perfect the way I am, but there is always room for improvement. We are all perfect the way we are because that is how God made us. We just need to see what we can do to make our lives and others' lives better. So, I am perfect the way I am, I strive to get better no matter what, and I am always grateful for the progress I make. There is only one true definition of perfection to me and that is acceptance. If I realize that this world is the way that God wants it to be, then we are all perfect the way we are. That and we can always strive for a better awareness.

"I thought that there was something inside me, and inside everyone, that was evil in one way or another. I thought there had to have been because I looked around the world and I saw a lot of chaos. I have now come to believe because of a different professor I had in college. He told me that fear, anger, and other character defects that are in me, and in us all, are not things. They are just absence of good. He said this came from the Neoplatonists. This professor told me that evil is not a thing. He described it like a hole in a sock. The whole is not a thing. It is an absence of sock. He told me that Pseudo-Dionysius wrote: 'by aspiring to the non-existent we aspire to evil.' The sock can be repaired. We all can. This is why they are just defects of character like it tells us.

"This is what the Twelve Steps have done for me, and because of Al-Anon I have acceptance of everyone. Even the people that wronged me, or the ones that I don't think are doing it right, for how do I really know? I'm not too conventional when it comes to recovery, so I am going to use a quote from the greatest of the Neoplatonists, Plotinus. The topic today with the meeting is: the giver is not aware of the gift, but simply gives. This to me is what it means to love, and the best way to give that gift, is just to love as many as I can without expectation. Thank you."

As the room applauded, I was trying to hide my tears. He spoke to me. I realized that I just wanted to control Jessica. I wanted her to have my values, and this was what was causing all of my problems. I needed to accept her and let her go.

The meeting went on. I usually share at every AA meeting I go to, but at this meeting I was just listening and relating. I knew I had to detach from her. It was the only truth that was ringing in my ears and moving my heart. As people were sharing, I pulled out my cell phone. People aren't supposed to text in meetings, but I knew that I had to detach from her, and I knew that I needed to do it now.

I entered her number into the texting screen of my phone, and then I wrote, "Jessica, I love you, and I haven't been showing you that well. I've been trying to control you. I have been trying to get you sober, and I now know I don't have that power. I can't get you sober. That is up to you. I want the best for you, so that is why I need to let you live your life. I wish you the best, and I hope that you learn everything you need to in this lifetime. I can't see you again. I am just making things worse for you and me. Take care, and I hope you find what you need."

After that, I blocked the number from my phone. I would never let myself cry in front of people, but at this meeting, and this particular time, I couldn't stop.

When the meeting was over we all held hands and said the Serenity Prayer, just as they do in all twelve-step meetings. I didn't know what I was going to do next, but I was starting to feel at peace because I could accept that I didn't know. I truly didn't know, and every time in my life when I could pray to those words, I started to get some clarity. It had never been so clear to me as it was at that moment that if I wanted love, I needed to give it to all. No matter what someone does today, I can realize that when it is either vicious or kind, it is beyond their control. All I should do is accept them and try my hardest to do the next right thing. Like I have been taught in recovery, I can live a better life.

"I try, I practice, I cultivate" is what they have all told me. This is how I repair the hole in the sock, and this is what I saw right then that I need to take into all areas of my life. I give the others in my life the love and acceptance that I have always longed for. Since I have given it to them, I have finally got it in return.

I heard a quote from Aquinas one time that said, "When wisdom comes to man, it is man that changes and not wisdom." To me the wisdom that I have always been looking for was how to give and receive love. Today, because of recovery, I give it my all to love all people, even the ones I can't stand. I'm not perfect at this. I make mistakes constantly, but I know what it is that I should strive for and how to always aim higher. When it comes to powerlessness, I am truly powerless over everything. It is fighting to gain control that has led to all of my conflicts. Once I could admit my powerlessness, I have been able to surrender and be gently guided to do the next right thing. I have taken a lot of the conflict out of my life by trying to practice this with everyone. It has been shown to me over and over that the road of life is very complicated, but the answer is always simple: wanting the best for someone, and taking the necessary steps to carry that out. That is just love and acceptance.

Once when I was sitting in silent mediation, I realized that I always speak up so much because I just want to be loved. I never had a good sense of self-worth before Al-Anon because I was always getting attention and love confused. I have always been good at proving to others that I am superior to them through my insults, but when I was meditating I realized that need for superiority was based on fear—the fear of not being enough and fear of how I was compared to how they were. I shouldn't judge another on our superficial differences. The most important things about ourselves are identical. That's when it came to me that if I want love, all I should do is give it to everyone, just like it tells all of us in the prayer of Saint Francis.

Epilogue: Truth and Happiness

I am writing this book in my junior year at SFSU. I was first going to go into accounting because of the bookkeeping job that I was at while I was living this story, but it wasn't my love. As a child, I wanted to be a writer. I could barely read because of my Asperger's, and I have been a functional illiterate most of my adult life. Even when I first started doing bookkeeping I could barely read, but today, and because of recovery, both from alcohol and other the struggles I've had with other people, I am living all of my dreams. I was trapped on SSDI for 15 years, but now my life is about fulfilling my dreams. I am completely off of disability, I have gotten one college degree, and now I am going for another in philosophy. This is why I wrote this book.

Taking the required class to be able to graduate, I needed to write a final essay, and I thought it would go well as an epilogue to this book. In another book: *True to Life, Why Truth Matters,* by Michael P Lynch, Lynch talks about truth and happiness. Two of Lynch's main ideas is that people want the truth, and truth matters to everyone. I completely disagree with the concept that people want the truth. If truth truly matter to everyone, then everyone would have an open mind. If everyone had an open mind, then people would be doing everything they could to get every answer possible. If people did everything they could to get every answer possible, I wouldn't see the need for any kind of war or conflict in any way. War and conflict itself are about values, and people expecting other people to value what they value. If everyone had an open mind, and they all sought the truth, then we would all be searching for the same universal values. This is clearly not what happens, and this is shown in my book. Jessica and I had different values, and I couldn't accept the fact that we did. Because I couldn't accept it, I had the problems that I had with her and everyone else in my life.

It would be nice if everyone wanted what was true, but what people want is to know that what they hold as true, and what they value, is true. Instead of seeking what is true, people want to know that they are right. People tell themselves that they want the truth, but the only reason they tell themselves they want the truth, without truly wanting it, is because of pride and ego. It is ego that is the only problem that I think we truly have, and this is why it is important to "Know thyself," as Socrates would say.

In the book, *Greek Thought and the Origins of the Scientific Spirit,* Leon Robbin writes that Socrates said, "The passionate man and the vicious man are men who do not know their own good. Men who have not perceived the essence of man in themselves. No one is willingly wicked. Reciprocally, virtue is another branch of knowledge; to know is to do." This is what tells me that when people do wrong things it is because they are ignorant. This was one of the main premises in my book. I was completely ignorant of why I was so cruel to people. I did not see what was driving my behavior, and I really didn't change until I did.

When people are ignorant about themselves, which from what I have seen most are, there are all kinds of problems in the world. Every problem that we have with human behavior is because we don't know who we are. I don't believe in bad people. I believe in ignorant people. It was my ego that drove me, and I have seen that same ego in other people's behavior to varying degrees. The qualities of my ego manifest and are driven by three different motivations: validation, gratification, and justification.

I wanted the validation of Jessica's love. I wanted the gratification to be able to feel superior to anyone, which I have always been extremely good at, and when I did conquer someone, I always justified it. These were the three things that have controlled me for most of my life, and it wasn't until I was willing to search for what was true that I stopped that behavior. Validation, gratification, and justification are what make up my ego. I believe they make up all our egos. I still have a big ego that I am trying to overcome. I have gotten a lot better, but I still love showing people how smart I am. My wife tells me that I am Iron Man without the super powers because I'm intelligent, I know it, and I'm an asshole about it. My wife tells me all the time that I am not humble, and the only reason I am this way is because I have felt so inferior my whole life. This part of me is nothing but ego, and ego is fear.

I agree with Lynch that truth is something that matters for its own sake, but the only truth that can't be questioned to me is: that one, I exist; and two, I can always be wrong. Everything else about this world is all probability and speculation. The only thing that I can know is myself, and the amazing thing is that I have come to believe that there is no difference between me and anyone else.

Sigmund Freud said humans have two driving forces that control our behavior: sex and a need for importance. These were the driving forces of me in this story. It is this need of importance that I see in myself and everyone else's behavior. It is this need of importance that was underneath the validation, gratification, and justification. This is why Lynch was right when he said self-knowledge is awareness. Lynch is also correct when he says that it is deep reflection that gets us to that awareness.

Most people, just by looking at myself and seeing it reflected to me in others' behavior, get their sense of importance by how they compare to the people around them. Who doesn't want to be the smartest or the best looking? Who doesn't what to have a higher social status than someone else? These are desires that we all live by until we can see that it is the only problem that we truly have. People have always told me I was intelligent. I heard it from all of my doctors and friends. The problem was that I always felt so stupid because I couldn't read and was terrible in school. This was the driving factor in my ego. I always felt less than. I defined myself on how I compared and what I thought others were thinking of me.

That problem with this is that we all define ourselves on what we think other people are thinking of us. That in itself is nothing but madness, and I am no different than anyone else because I have noticed others' motivations are the same as mine: To try and figure out what other people are thinking of me was the cause of my insanity. I took a class, philosophy of the mind, where one of the main ideas was that we can't even prove other people have minds, let alone what they are truly thinking. This is why I was so hostile. I was paranoid. I always focused on what people thought of me, and I always thought that it was something bad. I felt less than. The thing is, we all do this in one way or another.

Just last night I was listening to a speaker tell her story. She did the same thing that I have done so many times. I was never aware that that was what I was doing, and I don't think that she was aware of what she was doing right then either.

What she was doing was getting her sense of self by the response of the people listening to her. She wanted to take herself as important because she had been through so much. She was trying to get love from everyone by showing us how much she has overcome, and everything she was doing for charity. She was so attached to her past that it was still controlling her. This lady was an international speaker for the United Nations and had been through a lot, but to me she was blind to the message that she was giving. Her message to me was that she identified herself based on what the people in the room were thinking of her.

Lynch writes how "desires effectively guide our actions." The desire that was guiding her action was the desire to be loved. She wanted to be loved by everyone in the room. She was looking for approval from other people. I saw that, and I saw that it was myself reflected right back to me. I have been through more than most Americans from what others have told me as well. My suffering always gave me a feeling of importance when people told me that. I was better than others because I went through more, or I overcame so much more than everyone. Or even worse, I was better than because I was so much worse. For misery was one of the only things I had at one time. It was this sense of self that I got from what others told me. I needed to be important. I saw that in her, and it was just a projection of myself.

Lynch was doing the same thing when he wrote this book. Lynch's main purpose for writing his book is a higher status and to get people to admire him. He wants people to think that he knows what he is talking about. Anyone who writes a book, and puts their name to it, wants some type of notoriety. That is my reason for writing this book. I want people to see how mean I used to be, and how today I try to love everyone; therefore, Lynch is just me and every other writer. I'm not saying he doesn't have a love of truth, for that is what got him to be a philosopher. What I am saying is he wants some type of recognition.

Lynch writes, "Intuitively, what I most deeply care about helps to constitute my identity." This is the problem: what I think I know about myself. I like the prayer of Saint Francis where it says, "by self-forgetting one finds." My ego is my only problem, and that ego is always based on what I think another is thinking of me. It is not who I truly am, but the delusion of what I believe myself to be. It is madness to continue to focus on that, but it is something that we all do because we all want to be important in the eyes of others. Fear is what makes us "wicked." Most people never see this because of the they don't have any ability to reflect.

I agree with Lynch about how the good life is a matter of degree, at least for all except the avatars: Jesus, Pythagoras, Krishna, Empedocles, and the like. Yet who knows if they are anything more than just nebulous models to live our lives by. So yes, caring about truth is a necessary happiness for us all. Where I disagree with him is that it is something that we all want. We tell ourselves we want it, but a lot of us are in denial. What we want is to be important. If we looked into ourselves and saw our values for who we are, then we would want that truth. The problem with most humans is that we need to take ourselves as so unique that there is a fear that drives most of us. We get our importance about how much better or different than other people we are.

The fear that I had of others, and how I was seen in their eyes, was something that I was blind to most of my life. I was one of the angriest people that most had ever met, and I had no ability to see it. I always thought I was so courageous because I would never back down, but the only thing any of that was, was fear. It wasn't until I looked into myself and asked that "why" that Lynch mentions. That why is extremely important. Why is it that I am doing what I am doing? Is it based in ego? For ego is fear. It was this ego that got me to take myself as so much different. The only happiness I have gotten is by trying to give up all those things that I take about myself as unique. Sure, those desires manifest in different ways for all of us, but at the core there are only two: fear and love. That is not my idea. I had a friend tell me that, and this is proven with all of the current conflict in the world right now.

While I was writing this book, Donald Trump became president. I don't have any of the political views that Trump has; in fact, I take his as terrible, but he is someone that I relate to more than anyone else. I was never much of a liar, but I have had the same need of validation that he has. I see in this man someone who can never be enough. I see someone that has no ability to live up to his father, and for me that was my problem for a long time. My father was a college professor with a PhD in organic chemistry. I was so terrible is school that it drove me crazy. Trump isn't the businessman that his father was, and. Trump takes his feelings of inadequacy out on others just like I used to.

Trump is consumed with what people think of him. This is why he lashes out at everyone. He loves to humiliate people with his words, and he is blind to why he does it. He is driven by the need of validation. He wants to be great in other people's eyes. Why else would be call newspapers and pretend to be someone else just so they could report great things about him? He is controlled by the gratification of feeling superior to others, and he justifies all of his vicious actions.

I also see in Trump what I have always wanted. I wanted to be loved by everyone, and when I didn't think that people loved me, I thought that they hated me. If someone was going to hate me, I wanted to punish them. This was the problem. I always thought that everyone hated me, so I had to punish everyone. I was driven and consumed by fear just like he is. I am no longer that way today. I have also found it to be true that "to love is to be loved," just like it says in the prayer of Saint Francis.

Trump, just like I used to, gets attention and love confused. I always needed the gratification of feeling superior to people, and I did that with the attention I got from putting them down. So, I disagree with Lynch in the end about only giving a limited amount of love to a select few. From what I have seen, if I want to feel loved, then the only way I get it is to give it away. Not to a select few but to everyone. Love's not about something you get from another person. It is about the way it makes you feel to give it freely away; and the problem with the world is that not all of us have a good definition of love, and most of us only want to give it to a select few. For to me, love is wanting the best for someone and taking the necessary steps to carry that out. I can practice this with everyone today.

It doesn't mean I can solve anyone's problems because I can't. I am powerless over all people. It just means that no matter what, I accept them, and see what it is that I can truly do for another instead of thinking I know what is best. The point of this book was that it doesn't matter what anyone else does. It only matters what I do. This is where all my happiness lies. This has been what is true for me, and I hope it is shown to who all read this story. By seeing myself in everyone that crosses my path, I can infer it is true for them too; but again, the only thing I can truly know is myself.